For Ollie
Birthday 1983
from
Mutt & D.

AMERICA'S GRAND RESORT HOTELS

Pantheon Books, New York

AMERICA'S GRAND
RESORT HOTELS

Jeffrey Limerick, Nancy Ferguson and Richard Oliver
Designed by Janet Odgis

Graphic Credits

Art Director & Designer: Janet Odgis
Graphic Director: R. D. Scudellari
Production Director: Karen Bendelstein
Typesetting: Advertising Services, Inc.
Mechanicals: Libra Graphics
Printing: The Murray Printing Company
Binding: The Murray Printing Company

Library of Congress Cataloging in Publication Data
Limerick, Jeffrey.
America's grand resort hotels.
Bibliography: p.
Includes index.
1. Hotels, taverns, etc.   United States.
2. Architecture   United States. I. Ferguson.
Nancy, joint author. II. Oliver, Richard,
joint author. III. Title.
NA7840.L55   728.5   79-1885
ISBN 0-394-50107-1

Manufactured in the United States of America

First Edition

This book is dedicated to
Theodore Roosevelt and Edward, Prince of Wales,
those irrepressible resorters
without whom many grand hotels
would never have flourished.

Contents

Acknowledgments
A great many people have contributed to the making
of this book. They include hotel employees,
local historians, librarians, photographers,
architects, and devoted resorters, all of whom
shared their resources and their enthusiasms, and many of
whom have allowed us to publish materials in their care.
To all of them, we offer our thanks. We are also
grateful to our editor, Barbara Plumb, for her patience
and support and especially for this opportunity.

Map Key

WHITE CIRCLE: extant hotel, see hotel listing for location and telephone.

BLACK CIRCLE: extant building, but converted to another use, see hotel listing for location and telephone.

GRAY CIRCLE: hotel building no longer in existence.

1. Congress Hall, Saratoga Springs, New York.
2. Union Hall, Saratoga Springs.
3. Columbian, Saratoga Springs.
4. Pavilion, Saratoga Springs.
5. Covent Garden, Saratoga Springs.
6. Sans Souci, Ballston Spa, New York.
7. Atlantic Hall, Cape May, New Jersey.
8. Congress Hall, Cape May.
9. Mansion House, Cape May.
10. Mount Vernon, Cape May.
11. Catskill Mountain House, New York.
12. Grand Central (Old White), White Sulphur Springs, West Virginia.
13. Grand Union, Saratoga Springs.
14. United States, Saratoga Springs.
15. Continental, Long Branch, New Jersey.
16. Ocean House, Long Branch.
17. Mansion House, Long Branch.
18. Hotel Raymond, Pasadena, California.
19. Mohonk Mountain House, New Paltz, New York.
20. Poland Spring House, Poland Spring, Maine.
21. Wentworth-by-the-Sea, Portsmouth, New Hampshire.
22. The Balsams, Dixwell Notch, New Hampshire.
23. Manhattan Beach Hotel, Coney Island, New York.
24. Brighton Beach Hotel, Coney Island.
25. Oriental Hotel, Coney Island.
26. Grand Hotel, Mackinac Island, Michigan.
27. Grove Park Inn, Asheville, North Carolina.
28. Battery Park Inn, Asheville.
29. Kenilworth, Asheville.
30. Ponce de Leon, Saint Augustine, Florida.
31. Alcazar, Saint Augustine.
32. Tampa Bay Hotel, Tampa, Florida.
33. The Royal Poinciana, Palm Beach, Florida.
34. Belleview-Bitmore Hotel, Belleair, Florida.
35. Hotel Del Monte, Monterey, California.
36. Hotel Del Coronado, Coronado, California.
37. Saltair, Great Salt Lake, Utah.
38. Montezuma Hotel, Las Vegas Hot Springs, New Mexico.
39. El Tovar, Grand Canyon National Park, Arizona.
40. Alvarado Hotel, Albuquerque, New Mexico.
41. La Fonda Hotel, Santa Fe, New Mexico.
42. Old Faithful Inn, Yellowstone National Park, Wyoming.
43. Canyon Hotel, Yellowstone National Park.
44. Lake McDonald Lodge, Glacier National Park, Montana.
45. Glacier Park Lodge, Glacier National Park.
46. Many Glacier Hotel, Glacier National Park.
47. The Greenbrier, White Sulphur Springs, West Virginia.
48. Paradise Inn, Mount Rainier, Washington.
49. The Antlers, Colorado Springs, Colorado.
50. Hotel Colorado, Glenwood Springs, Colorado.
51. Marlborough-Blenheim Hotel, Atlantic City, New Jersey.
52. Hotel Traymore, Atlantic City.
53. The Broadmoor, Colorado Springs, Colorado.
54. The Breakers, Palm Beach, Florida.
55. Cloister Inn, Boca Raton, Florida.
56. Flamingo Hotel, Miami Beach, Florida.
57. Nautilus Hotel, Miami Beach.
58. Biltmore Hotel, Miami Beach.
59. Pancoast Hotel, Miami Beach.
60. King Cole Hotel, Miami Beach.
61. Boulevard Hotel, Miami Beach.
62. Floridian Hotel, Miami Beach.
63. Roney Hotel, Miami Beach.
64. Deauville Casino, Miami Beach.
65. Hotel Rolyat, Saint Petersburg, Florida.
66. Santa Barbara Biltmore, Montecito, California.
67. Beverly Hills Hotel, Beverly Hills, California.
68. Mission Inn, Riverside, California.
69. Arizona Biltmore, Phoenix, Arizona.
70. The Ahwahnee, Yosemite National Park, California.
71. Timberline Lodge, Mount Hood, Oregon.
72. Royal Hawaiian Hotel, Honolulu, Hawaii.
73. Madonna Inn, San Luis Obispo, California.
74. Habitation Le Clerc, Haiti.
75. Sun Valley, Idaho.
76. Polynesian Hotel, Walt Disney World, Orlando, Florida.
77. Contemporary Hotel, Walt Dsney World, Orlando.
78. Sans Souci Hotel, Miami Beach.
79. Fontainebleau Hotel, Miami Beach.
80. Eden Roc Hotel, Miami Beach.
81. Americana Hotel, Miami Beach.
82. Caesar's Palace, Las Vegas, Nevada.
83. MGM Grand, Las Vegas.
84. Aladdin Hotel, Las Vegas.
85. Stardust Hotel, Las Vegas.
86. Flamingo Hotel, Las Vegas.
87. Circus Circus, Las Vegas.
88. Mauna Kea, Hawaii.
89. Tahara'a Intercontinental, Papeete, Tahiti.
90. Playboy Resort Hotel, Lake Geneva, Wisconsin.
91. Kah-Nee-Ta Lodge, Warm Springs, Oregon.
92. Camino Real, Cancún, Mexico.
93. Galveston Beach Hotel, Galveston, Texas.
94. Caneel Bay Plantation, Saint John, Virgin Islands.
95. Essex House, Miami Beach
96. New Yorker Hotel, Miami Beach

Maine

20
22

New Hampshire
21

Wisconsin

26

1 2
4 5 3
6
13 14
Michigan

New York
11

19

23
15 24
16 25
17
New Jersey
52
51
7 8
9
10

West Virginia 97
12
47
Virginia

North Carolina

28
29
27

90

America's Grand
Resort Hotels

Florida 30
31

76
77

65 32

34

33
54

55
56 60 61 62
57
58 63 64 78 79
59 80 81 95 96

Texas 93

Themes & Images

Grand resort hotels constitute an architectural genre that both mirrors American culture and embodies many American values. The very words "grand resort hotel" bring to mind summer fancies and sporting revelry amidst a splendid setting. The history of resort life presents a cross section and a record of American social, cultural, and architectural development. By looking at resorts, one can appreciate the impact of new means of transportation and technological innovations; the American attraction to novelty and fashion; the changes in American attitudes toward nature and the landscape; and the connection between architectural styles and cultural aspirations.

From colonial times to the present, Americans have traveled to the seashore, into the wilderness, and to mineral springs in search of renewed health, spiritual enlightenment, aesthetic catharsis, or merely a change of pace. Resorts have also given Americans an opportunity to mingle with people of similar interests and of similar social standing—or of that to which they aspired. The patrons of grand resort hotels have included business tycoons, political leaders, socialites, fortune-hunters, and even a few unsavory scoundrels. For some people, part of the attraction of going to a resort lies in the opportunity to observe these famous folks at play. In the nineteenth and early twentieth centuries, the resort hotel was one place where wealthy Americans could spend lavishly as proof of their hard-earned material success. In those earlier times, it was like a stage for the display of its patrons. While the ability to attract notable guests still contributes to the fame of a hotel, most resort-goers today prefer anonymity: their chief purpose is neither to see nor to be seen, but merely to enjoy a relaxing break in their daily routine. Now that wealth is no insurance against violence, the wealthy often seek resorts that offer privacy and insularity, from other resorters as well as

from the outside world. The modern counterparts of the Vanderbilts and the Astors usually choose to patronize places that are more like secluded, walled gardens than like flamboyant stage sets. Yet the flashier and more public resort hotels—direct descendants of the nineteenth-century palaces—still exist for an upper-middle-class clientele.

Exclusivity continues to hold an allure for many Americans, and a successful resort must still have an aura of exclusiveness. Happily, the odious discrimination that arose when resorters' prejudices of race and religion tightly circumscribed the group with which they wished to associate is now largely a thing of the past. Of course, the prospect of flirtation and romance has been one of the consistent social attractions of resort life. For participant and spectator alike, resort hotels provide an arena for social games of every sort.

Although the costumes and habits of resorters have changed through the years, many of the specific activities of resort life have remained remarkably constant. An example is the urge people on vacation have to dance in the late afternoon. The tea dance, as this event is invariably called, is an opportunity to socialize, to engage in flirtation, to arrange a date for dinner, or simply to cap off the afternoon's more sporting activities. In the resort towns along Fire Island in the late 1970s, couples gather to dance to the latest disco hits, recalling the frenetic couples of the Jazz Age who danced to Paul Whiteman's orchestra at tea dances in the Oriental Tea Garden of the Flamingo Hotel in Miami. Similarly, earlier resort-goers assembled for thés dansants in the Coconut Grove of the Royal Poinciana Hotel in Palm Beach at the turn of the century, and for the afternoon hop at White Sulphur Springs in the 1860s.

While we discuss the social, historical, and even nostalgic aspects of a number of resort hotels, our

A Shingle Style hotel like many on the New England shore, at Manhattan Beach near Los Angeles, circa 1895

primary purpose is to consider these buildings as significant and serious works of architecture, and not merely as period pieces or curiosities. Each hotel we present was designed to answer the needs of a particular time and place and to live up to the expectations of a particular clientele. Yet the world of the resort hotel is also extremely fragile. Hotels have been vulnerable to financial disaster, to the whims of a fickle, fashion-conscious patronage, and, especially in the nineteenth century, to fire. Those that survive from the nineteenth and early twentieth centuries have done so because they were able to accommodate changes in fashion, taste, social mores, and economic conditions. Like all great buildings, they both mirror their own time and embody more timeless qualities of architecture.

Resort hotels must possess two seemingly contradictory architectural characteristics. On one hand, they must be efficient machines designed for the systematic provision of meals, clean rooms, and other services by an inconspicuous staff. They must serve their guests handsomely while rendering a profit to their owners. On the other hand, they must embody some popular image of the good life. Whether festive stage sets or deliberately reclusive settings, they must offer an environment that is distinct from the everyday urban world of most resort-goers.

As models of comfort and efficiency, hotels have

introduced numerous conveniences and technological innovations to the American public. In the nineteenth century, steam heat, gas and electric lights, modern plumbing, elevators, and box-spring mattresses became familiar to resort hotel patrons before they were commonplace in American homes. This concern with providing services and luxuries that are up-to-the-minute is a part of the competitive nature of the hotel business. Yet these conveniences are but one aspect of luxury that pervades a truly grand resort hotel.

Much of the appeal of these hotels, both as places to visit and as objects of study, rests in their creation of a unique and often fanciful setting. Resort hotels have been modeled on Bavarian lodges, log cabins, Spanish farmhouses. Italian palazzi, South Pacific villages, and antebellum Southern mansions. These prototypes have been interpreted with varying degrees of fidelity or capriciousness. The particular theme chosen for a resort building is often inspired by and intended to complement the natural setting or local history. In Florida, for example, hotel developers sought to create an American Riviera, aided by an architectural style based on Spanish, Italian, and Moorish images and forms. Glacier Park emphasized its associations with the Alps through the use of Swiss-inspired buildings. Not only does the landscape influence the appearance of resort hotels; it also can be the very reason for their construction. Since the

The swimming pool and sun deck of the Ivanhoe Hotel in Miami Beach

early nineteenth century, enterprising hotel builders have capitalized on raging waterfalls, precipitous cliffs, and smooth beaches for their success in attracting vacationers. Even as society has become more urbanized, the wilder side of nature continues to have an enormous allure. But with the exception of the earliest wilderness hostels, the tourist's experience of nature has always been tempered by the comfort and luxury of the resort hotel itself.

As conservative business ventures, resort hotels have never been in the vanguard of architectural style. Rather, they have been composed of images familiar enough to their patrons to put them at ease, yet novel enough to hold their attention and to reinforce the notion that the hotel is a special place. Because of their freedom from restricted urban sites, and because their purpose is to delight, hotels have had license to exaggerate, both in scale and image. Aside from their other unique features, their tremendous size was enough to set them off from everyday experience. Few buildings of any sort could rival the hotels of Saratoga Springs, whose porches were measured by the mile and whose gardens were measured by the acre. Even today, the MGM Grand Hotel in Las Vegas takes pride in possessing a casino that is larger than a football field. But at the best resort hotels, gigantic scale does not imply an impersonal atmosphere. Part of

the pleasure in staying at such places resides in the feeling that the vast and luxurious spaces were created expressly for one's own enjoyment.

The earliest American resort hotels were little more than country inns or taverns, and they posed no architectural problems that the local house builder could not solve. But as the nineteenth century progressed, the increased size and complexity of resort hotels fostered the development of resort specialists, including architects and interior designers, food and laundry experts, and professional managers. The colorful figures who once operated their own hotels have by and large been replaced by corporate owners.

In the following pages, we present a number of notable resort hotels. We have tried to select buildings that reflect three of the most important characteristics of the genre: the landscape setting—seashore, springs, or scenic wilderness; the method of transportation most commonly used to reach them—steamboat and horse-and-buggy, railroad, automobile, or airplane; and evolving architectural fashions. Limited space has forced us to leave out many wonderful examples; to their devotees, our apologies. We have, finally, attempted to capture a sense of the life of this fascinating and disquieting world, with its balance of tradition and innovation, propriety and eccentricity.

Early History of the Hotel

The hotel as a building type first appeared in the late 1700s as a larger version of the traditional inn, offering facilities suited to formal social life in addition to providing food and lodging for man and horse. While the inn predates Biblical times, by the Middle Ages some European examples had grown in comfort, if not elegance, to the point where their patrons occasionally included royalty. Travel—the raison d'être of the inn—kept pace with increasing mercantile activity, encouraging accommodations to grow both in size and in sophistication. In his History of Building Types, Sir Nikolaus Pevsner mentions several German establishments that had reached hotel size by 1700. In 1770, Dessien's hôtel (the French word for a large house or mansion) in Calais was reportedly a small town in itself with squares, gardens, shops, and a theater. The birth of the hotel, then, came when dining rooms, ballrooms, and spaces for assembly were added to older inns or designed as an integral part of new ones, to accommodate the social activities that centered there and to offer the facilities of the private palace to those of less than royal means.

The inns of colonial America followed the example of the simple country inns of England. Most of them were converted from private residences, with one main room that served as parlor, dining room, and bar. Here meals were taken with the host and his family. Indoor sanitary facilities and private rooms were still idle dreams of the weary traveler. Washing was usually done in the kitchen or out by the stable-yard pump. The moral objection to strangers of different sexes occupying the same room was overcome by the host's flat refusal to admit a woman unaccompanied by a husband or a parent.

Uncomfortable and inconvenient as they sound to us, American inns were, like their European counterparts, centers of community life. Here business was transacted, gossip exchanged, letters posted, and friendships formed or broken. City hostelries were merely larger versions of those in smaller towns; most of them were still converted residences with additions. But as travel increased and the number of patrons grew, some buildings were erected specifically for the accommodation of travelers. The first to call itself a hotel, after the European example, was New York's City Hotel of 1794, with an eye-popping 73 rooms. It quickly became the scene of important banquets and weekly subscription dances where fashionable Knickerbockers gathered in gowns, knee breeches, silk stockings, and white dancing gloves to try the latest French cotillion or allemande.

Within a decade, large inns like the City Hotel appeared in other American cities. The most interesting, to judge from contemporary descriptions, was Boston's Exchange Coffee House of 1807, designed by Asher Benjamin. It was seven stories tall, with a commerical exchange, a dining room, a ballroom, and guest chambers disposed on galleries overlooking a five-story interior court, topped by a dome nearly 100 feet in diameter with a central glass skylight. This building anticipated the current fad for vast lobby spaces by nearly 160 years.

American efforts in the development of the hotel remained secondary to those in Europe. Nevertheless, one of the most advanced designs of this period was proposed for Richmond, Virginia, in 1797 by Benjamin Latrobe, who later helped to design the United States Capitol. He had just arrived in this country from his native England when he prepared the plan, which featured an elegant assembly room and guest rooms on either side of a grand semi-domed theater. Within a few years, buildings of similar design had been built in Europe, notably John Foulson's Royal Hotel and Athenaeum in Plymouth, England,

Boston's famous Tremont House of 1829

which had grand Greek-columned porticoes to mark its entrances. However, it was not until 1829, with the opening of the Tremont House in Boston, that the United States stepped into the lead in the development of the modern hotel.

The Tremont was the first hotel to become an architectural monument. Isaiah Rogers, its young architect, had given a good deal of thought to the improvement of hotel design. The Tremont offered the public some surprises. There was no traditional sign or hitching post to mar the chaste beauty of its classical Greek façade. Upon entering, the guest found himself, not in a barroom, but rather in a columned rotunda intended specifically as an office and lobby. The bar was now in an elegant room of its own, one of ten high-ceilinged, marble-floored public rooms sumptuously decorated in the latest French style. The cuisine matched the decor. The dining room was gigantic for those days (70 by 31 feet), and in a squeeze could accommodate 200 diners at one sitting. Other public rooms could be used for meetings and parties, and could be enlarged through the use of sliding doors. A subscription library supplied hotel guests and library members with books and newspapers.

Guests could hardly believe the luxury of private rooms, carpeted floors, lockable doors, and the free use of a cake of yellow soap. The privies and eight bathing rooms were actually indoors, located at the rear of the courtyard, which was now devoted to a garden rather than to the care of horses.

The Tremont House was hailed by the normally restrained Bostonians as "one of the triumphs of American genius." It was not long before other hotels began to imitate its features, aided by a book on the building which became the unofficial handbook of hotel design for the next several decades. Rogers himself was soon hired to best his early efforts. His Astor House, built in New York for fur trader and real estate king John Jacob Astor, was two stories taller, had nearly twice as many rooms, and was even more elegantly furnished than its predecessor. In addition, the incorporation of a new steam pump allowed water to be raised to privies and bathing rooms on the upper floors.

The basis for competition among American hotels was now established. Within the limits of economic feasibility, they grew larger, kept abreast of the fashions in architecture and interior decoration, and introduced the public to the latest in convenience technology. Of course, the Tremont House and the Astor House quickly became outmoded. The latter survived only forty years before falling prey to the wrecker's ball. It was some time before hotels comparable to the city hotels appeared at American resorts. There were not enough vacationers to support such an in-

vestment until the 1830s, when improved travel conditions made resorts accessible to the leisured well-to-do.

America's early resorters must have been a hardy lot, for it was an arduous task to move family and supplies to mineral springs or to the shore. Yet it was worth the effort to find a comfortable climate and to escape from the epidemics of yellow fever and cholera that routinely racked the cities and inland lowlands each summer. Of course, such summer migrations were hardly a new phenomenon. The Pharaohs of Egypt used to celebrate the annual flooding of the Nile at the summer temple at Luxor. Renaissance popes and cardinals, following a well-established tradition, built elaborate retreats and gardens in the hills outside Rome. Also, from earliest times man has made use of mineral springs for their alleged curative powers. In Greece, India, Egypt, and Persia, springs were associated with the worship of gods and placed in the care of priests. The ancient Romans regarded spring bathing as a social occasion. Julius Caesar was an habitué of Vichy.

By the time the American colonies were settled, health resorts at European springs such as Wiesbaden, Spa, Bath, Tunbridge Wells, and Saint-Moritz were already well established and fully equipped to provide the pleasures and luxuries to which their wealthy and famous patrons were accustomed. When colonists discovered similar mineral springs enjoyed by American Indians, they began to emulate the yearly migrations fashionable in England. The Indians soon found themselves displaced.

It is difficult to say which was the first resort in America frequented by the white man. Stafford Springs near Hartford, Connecticut, was host to Yankee health-seekers in the late 1600s, and it was also one of the first resorts to fall from fashion. John King, a visitor there in 1840, found the place full of sad old bores "quaffing stupendous quantities of water."

Springs that were near Philadelphia—Yellow Springs, Bath, and Schooley's Mountain—became popular in the 1720s, and the springs of western Virginia first began to attract colonists in the 1750s. Whenever a spring was discovered that contained minerals such as iron, magnesium, or iodine, a health resort soon followed. Physicians wrote tomes extolling the virtues of one spring or another, claiming remarkable cures for ailments ranging from gout, the disease of aristocrats, to "female complaint." Whether the waters were actually beneficial is open to question. Dr. Benjamin Rush of Philadelphia, a famous colonial physician, considered the tonic effects of mineral waters merely a substitute for temperance and exercise, but he also believed the sensible diet, relaxation, and social life at the spring resorts to be salutary as well as enjoyable.

During these early years, springs were frequented by rich and poor alike. But as some resorts developed a reputation for attracting certain groups of people, resorters began to seek out their own kind, or at least the society they hoped to join. The springs became social centers where people ostensibly seeking health also discussed business and political affairs and pursued romance and relief from boredom.

While the Northern springs reflected the Puritan heritage of New England in their austere, religious tone, the Southern resorts were much more pleasure-oriented. On a preaching tour during the 1770s, the Reverend Philip V. Fithian found a great deal of excitement at Berkeley Springs in Virginia. Some four hundred people were there. The first night a fight erupted that left one of the combatants with a severely twisted nose. On another evening a splendid ball was held, and when Fithian walked out among the bushes he found that "amusements in all shapes and in high degrees were constantly taking place among so promiscuous a company." Cardplaying and billiards were also favorite pursuits in resort taverns during the 1780s and 1790s, and it was not unusual for a wealthy planter to arrive with a carriage and slaves and leave with only a horse.

Because of their easy accessibility, Northern resorts had good hotels long before decent accommodations were available at the Southern springs. George William Featherstonhaugh, the English geographer and author, arrived at White Sulphur Springs in 1834 to discover crowds of finely dressed ladies and gentlemen all struggling to find a place to stay in the crowded little village. Even if one succeeded in getting a roof over one's head, the food and lodgings were abominable. Four years later, the Reverend Alexander Wilson, of Charleston, South Carolina, described White Sulphur Springs as "decidedly the meanest, most nasty place in point of filth, dust and every other bad quality" that he had ever seen. At night he was alternately plagued by fleas and awakened by the grunting of hogs. Yet there he was, hundreds of miles by horse and stage from home, enduring great discomfort in search of a healthy respite, a change of pace, and a chance to mix with the Southern elite at the springs.

The tennis pavilion and courts at Hot Springs, Virginia

Above: The Putnam family's growing Union Hall (left) and Congress Hall (right). Below: Guests in Union Hall's garden

Early Resorts in America
SARATOGA SPRINGS
New York

Saratoga Springs was the most popular of America's nineteenth-century spas. The story of its founding and rise to national prominence is in many ways typical of such resorts. Almost from its start, Saratoga was the model other watering places sought to emulate.

The springs were discovered in 1767 by Sir William Johnson, the British Crown's representative to the Iroquois and an enthusiastic admirer of Indian ways — to the point, it is said, of fathering nearly a hundred children by Indian women. Legend has it that he was carried to the Indians' secret spring to heal a wound he had received battling the French near Lake George. After Johnson recovered, word of the cure and the amazing spring spread far and wide. After the Revolutionary War, wealthy Philip Schuyler blazed a trail to these springs from his estate near Albany, New York, and laid claim to them. Among the many visitors to try Schuyler's waters was George Washington, who considered buying the springs and building a summer house there. Nothing came of it, however, because the trip was still arduous and the comforts few. Schuyler had built a small guest cottage there, but visitors were obliged to bathe in a crude trough of the sort used to slop hogs.

Improved conditions came about only after Gideon Putnam, a young New Englander who had set up a logging operation and lumber mill nearby, realized that his resource of trees would soon be gone. The increasing numbers of visitors and the discovery of a new spring christened "The Congress" seemed to offer a golden opportunity. Putnam bought land around the Congress Spring and erected a three-story tavern and guesthouse. The building was 70 feet long, with two parlors, a dining room, and a kitchen on the main floor, and accommodations for 70 people on the floors above. The tavern proved so successful that it eventually had to be doubled in size to accommodate the throngs of health-seekers. When Putnam discovered that the bubbling mineral waters attracted people of means and some sophistication, he purchased more land and planned a village of broad, tree-lined streets. His final improvement was a hotel called the Congress Hall in honor of his spring. Unfortunately, he died as the result of a fall from its scaffolding in 1812, before it was completed. The old tavern was renamed Union Hall, and the Putnam family carried on the business.

Saratoga's initial success was not long-lasting. Competition grew as enterprising businessmen developed watering places at mineral springs from the mountains of western Virginia and Pennsylvania to New England. Besides, Saratoga's citizens were too straitlaced to provide amusements to complement the attraction of the waters. The dull routine of hymn singing, buggy rides, prayer, and taking the waters was even more strictly enforced after 1808, when the town became the home of America's first temperance society. Cards, dancing, and lively music were forbidden. Obviously, all but the most staid resorters went elsewhere, many to the springs at Ballston Spa only seven miles away.

Ballston Spa had been founded about the same time as Saratoga, and a tavern was built in the 1790s. A town was laid out and lots were sold, providing the developers with the money to build a hotel in 1803. Intended to outdo Gideon Putnam's tavern in Saratoga, the Sans Souci embodied architectural suggestions of the palace at Versailles, albeit much reduced in scale and opulence. Here is perhaps the first instance of a palace for a king being used as the image for a palace for the people. The hotel was built of pine. The central wing was 160 feet long, and two wings 153 feet long extended back to enclose a garden. This U-shaped plan around a garden was used for hotels throughout the nineteenth century. Extensive piazzas, or porches, faced both the street in front and the landscaped grounds in the rear. The Sans Souci boasted a French chef of great talent — a rare treat, as hotel food was often plentiful but usually quite ordinary and poorly prepared.

The building cost $60,000, a goodly sum in those days. On August 20, 1805, agriculturist and merchant Elkanah Watson returned to Ballston after a visit some years earlier and described in his journal the overnight success of the spa:

[We] reached the Sans Souci at Ballston, amid scenes of elegance and gaiety. We seated outselves at a sumptuous table, with about one hundred guests of all classes, but generally, from their appearance and deportment, of the first respectability, assembled here from every part of the Union and Europe, in the pursuit of health or pleasure, of matrimony or vice. This is the most splendid water place in America and scarcely surpassed in Europe in its dimensions and the taste and elegance of its arrangements. In the evening, we attended a ball in a spacious hall, brilliantly illuminated with chandeliers, and adorned with various other appliances of elegance and luxury. Here was congregated a fine exhibition of the beau monde. A large proportion of the assembly was from the Southern States, and distinguished by their elegant and polished manners. In the place of the old-fashioned country dances and four-hand reels of Revolutionary days, I was pleased to notice the advance of refined customs, and the introduction of the graces of Paris in the elegant cotillion and quadrille. At table I was delighted in observing the style and appearance of the company, males and females intermixed in the true French usage of sans souci. The board was supplied with the luxuries of more sunny climes. There was a large display of servants, handsomely attired, while the music of a choice band enlivened the festivities.

Everyone was impressed. Ballston soon hosted 2,000 guests a season, including such famous figures as Joseph Bonaparte (the deposed king of Spain and a brother of Napoleon) and Governor Clinton of New York.

Faced with dire economic prospects, the town fathers of Saratoga decided that at least some concessions to the devil would have to be made. About 1820, the Congress Hall added billiard rooms. Rides in the countryside no longer required chaperones. An orchestra provided music for dancing. Gentlemen were permitted to gamble at cards in the privacy of their rooms. Some of the old-timers were outraged, but the return of tourists in ever greater numbers allowed most of the residents to tolerate—even welcome—the compromise. Those who found the town's new worldliness a bit too sinful simply began to frequent other resorts where a more religious tone still prevailed. Eventually this led to the founding of a number of religious retreats such as those at Lake Chautauqua in New York and Ocean Grove in New Jersey, where strictly enforced rules and covenants kept Satan at bay.

Although Saratoga was still far from being the glamorous, sophisticated, and wicked place that its growing reputation suggested, guidebooks could note that "the minerals of Saratoga and the healing virtues of its Springs are not the only nor the principal objects which draw to its sands the thousands who annually flock thither." Saratoga sustained a lively rivalry with Ballston Spa for years, but the latter finally faded from fashion. The fortunes of the Sans Souci declined year by year. The hotel was first converted into a school of law and then into a ladies' seminary. Saratoga reigned supreme.

Because of its new attractions, Saratoga Springs became a featured stop on the Northern summer tour, the pattern for which had become established by 1820. Travelers started from New York City, guidebook in hand, and proceeded to Ballston or to Saratoga, stopping in the Catskill Mountains and making short excursions to Glens Falls and Lake George. Then at the end of the summer they returned by way of Niagara Falls, the Great Lakes, Portland, Maine, Boston, or whatever route was in favor that year. All this was made possible by greatly improved transportation. Steamboats began to ply the Hudson from New York to Albany in the early 1820s and were continually improved to lessen the hazards of accidents or explosions. Coaches ran from Albany to Saratoga twice daily in season. In addition, stages connected with canal boats bound for Boston at Fort Edward and with the steamers on Lake George.

Hotels in Saratoga expanded, and new ones were built to handle the crowds. Putnam's Union Hall grew to 120 feet in length, with two wings each extending back 60 feet. The Congress Hall, already 200 feet long and three stories high, added a north wing 100 feet in length. The Columbian, surrounded on three sides by gardens, also made improvements and additions. The Pavilion Hotel was built in 1819 to compete with the Congress Hall for the fashionable trade. A number of high-class boardinghouses could handle about 700 guests. When Elias Benedict built his United States Hotel in 1824, adding accommodations for 150, the demand for rooms was still greater than the supply.

As large as these buildings were, they were only larger versions of the traditional inn or boardinghouse. For example, the long rectangular first-floor space of the Congress Hall was simply partitioned into three rooms: a dancing hall 80 feet long, a dining room in the middle, and a ladies' parlor. The Pavilion had a similar arrangement, but through the use of folding doors all the rooms could open up into one vast space for large gatherings. The sleeping quarters on the floors above were cramped and hardly adequate for families. Rooms were often no larger than 6 feet square, with whitewashed walls and mat-covered

The fashionable United States was Saratoga's best hotel during the 1840s.

floors. Furnishings consisted of a bed, a bureau with
mirror, a washbowl and pitcher, a table, and two
chairs. Artificial light was provided by candles placed
at the head of the stairs for the guests to pick up on
the way to their rooms in the evening. Despite the
management's efforts to retrieve leftover bits of
candles for reuse, they were usually beaten to it by
gentlemen who sought to lay in a stock for late-night
parties and card games.

Those who felt the need of a bath had to visit one
of the nearby bathhouses on Broadway, where the
charge of 25 cents included the use of a towel and a
cake of soap. People were not too vexed about the
lack of bathing facilities; it was not common to bathe
very often. There were complaints about the crude
furniture and the inconvenient distance to a room in
the wings. But since accommodations were scarce
during the summer season, most people considered
themselves fortunate to have any sort of room at all.

While the gentlemen enjoyed card games in private
rooms, the ladies also demanded diversions. The
springs were scarcely enough to hold their attention,
especially as it became more and more obvious
that few people actually had any need of the waters.
Hotel managers arranged parlor games, hops, balls,
and concerts and hired lecturers, entertainers, and all

sorts of strolling players to amuse the guests. Cotillion
parties ranged in cost from $1.50 to $4.00, while the
"Champagne Balls" cost as much as $5.00. As early
as 1822, the two leading hotels, the Congress Hall
and the United States, shared the services of a band
of black musicians, which played alternately for tea
and dinner at each hotel. The manager of the Covent
Garden House, listing the attractions of his establishment in 1835, boasted of

**a fine garden laid out with great taste, and filled with a
variety of trees and shrubbery, in which can be had at
all times ice cream, confectionary, fruits, wines, and
other refreshments of the choicest kinds.**

**Also a great variety of amusements, such as
cosmorama, solar telescope, carousel, swing boat,
billiards, and bowling alleys.**

**The garden will be illuminated every evening, and con-
certs of music very frequently, in which boarders will
have free access.**

In addition, the guests themselves were the source
of a good deal of entertainment and spectacle. The
wives of Southern planters were constantly showing
off their latest Paris fashions and costly jewels. Not
to be outdone, the wives of wealthy New England
traders and businessmen responded in kind.

It was becoming increasingly clear that people were

coming to Saratoga for reasons other than health. English author and traveler James Silk Buckingham, who visited in 1838, makes a shrewd observation:

Saratoga affords perhaps the best opportunity that a stranger can enjoy for seeing American society on the largest scale, and embracing the greatest variety of classes at the same time; for except the small shop-keeper and mere labourer, every other class has its representative here. The rich merchant from New Orleans, the planter from Arkansas and Alabama, with the more haughty and polished landowner from the Carolinas and Virginia; the successful speculator in real estate from the West; the rich capitalist from Boston and New York; the official functionary from Washington; the learned professor from New Haven and Cambridge. The whole Union is thus brought before the eye of the stranger in one view.
Hundreds who, in their own towns, could not find ad-mittance into the circles of fashionable society there — for the rich and leading families of America are quite as exclusive as the aristocracy of England—come to Saratoga, where at Congress Hall or the United States, by the moderate payment of two dollars a day, they may be seated at the same table and often side by side with the first families of the country; promenade in the same piazza, lounge on the sofas in the same drawing-room and dance in the same quadrille with the most fashion-able beaux and belles of the land; and thus, for the week or month they may stay at Saratoga, they enjoy all the advantages which their position would make inacces-sible to them at home.

The social scene and the thrill of social contact had become the resort's prime attraction. Saratoga's town fathers were distressed by the mixing of classes, but chose to let the situation continue, for within what seemed a veritable melting pot a powerful process of differentiation was at work. Though the observer was tolerated, people associated mostly with their own kind. Hotels and boardinghouses began to be known for the sort of people they attracted. As the haunt of the conservative "Whig" aristocracy, the Congress Hall was a bit forbidding. The United States was the "Democratic" house, serving the mer-cantile class and the new rich. The Pavilion catered to short-term guests and transients. And the vener-able Union Hall, still run by the Putnam family, was a haven for clergymen, academics, judges, the devout, and the elderly.

The daily routine of life at Saratoga in the 1830s was a strange combination of charged, feverish ac-tivity and dawdling inertia. The day began at sunrise with a trip to the springs for a glass of mineral water at the Congress pavilion. Some overzealous health-seekers, taking a cure-or-kill attitude, might down twenty glasses of bubbling mineral water before breakfast.

Breakfast at the Saratoga hotels was a huge meal conducted in free-for-all boardinghouse fashion as people jostled to see who could get seats near whom and who could garner the choicest victuals. Consumed at breakneck speed, the whole prodigious offering of food was downed in no more than fifteen minutes. Dinner at one and tea at seven were much the same kind of affair. In such an atmosphere, fine cuisine would have been a waste of time, As Buckingham observed:

No fatigue during the day, or any other consideration, can induce persons to relax in the least from the hurry with which everything is done in this country [the States]. In the busy cities, the reason assigned for this haste is the keen pursuit of business, and the eager desire to get to the counting-house or store; but here, with the entire day before them, and nothing whatever to do, they eat with just the same haste as at other places. Elegance of manners in such a scene as this is quite out of the question.

By 1840, this began to change, as the practice of es-corting guests to their seats and serving better food in individual portions with military precision was adopted from the first "modern" city hotels. Meals then be-came much more leisurely and enjoyable parts of the daily routine.

After breakfast the visitor could enjoy the resort's amusements, though most chose to sink into a seden-tary torpor. Papers were read. Gossip was exchanged. Marriageable young ladies and gentlemen followed the rituals of courtship under the watchful eyes of their parents. Dinner at one was the event of the day, after which diners strolled the piazzas, seeing and being seen. An elaborate carriage procession to the countryside followed, allowing full show of clothing, fancy equipages, and fine horses. The evening meal was followed by more promenading, concerts, and entertainments. The day was usually capped by an in-formal hop or a stately ball, ending the evening in a flourish of activity and flirtation.

Saratoga was now firmly established as the leading American resort, rivaled only by Cape May and Newport. But the growing crowds, now arriving from Albany by railroad, brought problems as well as prosperity. It was not unusual to find several thousand people in town on any given day during the season. With so many strangers present, the restric-tions that confined gambling to private hotel rooms broke down. In 1842, the town's first public gambling house opened in an alley behind the United States Hotel. The citizens of Saratoga were uneasy about the presence of public gaming operations and shocked to discover that professional gamblers and criminal elements were soon in evidence. The resort town was acquiring those qualities of physical comfort and social complexity associated with the modern vacation. The scene was now set for the post-Civil War era, when Saratoga's prosperity and prominence would be based, not on mineral water, but on gambling, horse racing, and glittering self-display.

CAPE MAY
New Jersey

Even though Saratoga was America's most cosmopolitan resort, it was not the only popular spot. The seashore drew visitors for much the same reason as the springs: health, comfort, and later, social life.

The Jersey shore began to attract summer visitors around 1790, despite the fact that there were only a few ways to get there, all of them difficult. One could travel overland through the Pine Barrens from either Philadelphia or New York in freight vehicles known as "Jersey wagons." Before boardinghouses were established, visitors would carry stoves, blankets, food, and other supplies with them. Women seldom traveled this way; the trip was considered too long and too rough. As one traveler recalled, the Jersey wagon

seemed to have been designed by the Shakers in protest against every semblance of luxury or even comfort ... as free from graceful lines as those of a ready-made coffin.... [The springs were] cumbrous contrivances of unyielding wood so constructed as to make riding a weariness to the flesh and spirit.... [At the destination] the more robust were generally able to climb out but the feebler ones ... had to be lifted out.

Travel was considerably improved by the establishment of stage lines after 1816. Coaches left Camden at 4 a.m. and arrived at Cape May at midnight; 110 bone-jarring miles along a dusty dirt road were covered in twenty hours. One round trip a week operated between Philadelphia and Tuckerstown. By the 1830s, stages ran several times weekly on regular schedules.

Certainly the easiest and most popular way to reach shore points was by boat. Cape May was a leisurely two-day sail down the Delaware River from Philadelphia, including a stop at New Castle to take on passengers who had come overland from Baltimore or from the South. By the mid-1820s, steamship service had shortened the trip to one day. Many visitors also arrived aboard the cargo ships that sailed the coastal waters from Georgia to New England carrying agricultural goods north in the spring and returning with supplies and manufactured goods in late summer.

The travelers' trials were not over once they had arrived at the shore. As at the springs in early days, accommodations were crude and often inadequate. Visitors found lodging with the local farmers and fishermen. But as the shore became more popular, enterprising locals saw the possibility of turning a profit by providing better accommodations. In 1801, Postmaster Ellis Hughes of Cape Island advertised his Atlantic Hall in the Philadelphia Aurora as follows:

The public are respectfully informed that the subscriber has prepared himself for entertaining company who use sea bathing, and he is accommodated with extensive house room, with fish, oysters, crabs, and good liquor. Care will be taken of gentlemen's horses. The situation is beautiful, just at the confluence of the Delaware Bay with the ocean, in sight of the Light House, and affords a view of the shipping which enters and leaves the Delaware. Carriages may be driven along the margin of the ocean for miles, and the wheels will scarcely make an impression on the sand; the slope of the shore is so regular that persons may wade a great distance. It is the most delightful spot the citizens can retire to in the hot season.

This same building was also described as "a desolate barn of a place" by one of its patrons.

Cape May grew in popularity after the War of 1812. By the 1820s, a number of Philadelphians went there each summer to frolic in the surf, to enjoy the pleasures of the countryside, or to test their skill at hunting and fishing.

The Congress Hall, built in 1816 by Hughes's son Thomas, was as crude as its predecessors. It was a large wood-frame building three stories high with a tall veranda along one side, and without the least pretense of finish about it. Not an ounce of paint or plaster graced its rough board walls. Although uncomfortable by our standards, the Congress Hall was very popular, even after much more luxurious lodgings were available. The attraction of the shore and sea bathing kept it full year after year.

Enjoying a dip in the ocean was not a simple matter in those days. Bathing suits were bulky affairs

intended to stem all temptation by covering most of the body. Obviously, they made swimming very difficult. Most people just waded in about waist-deep and joyously jumped up and down. In most early resorts mixed bathing was frowned upon. A sign at the Mansion House in Cape May in 1839 read:

In order to prevent intrusion, a white Flag will be on the Bath House during the Ladies' hours and a red Flag for the Gentlemen.

Mrs. Frances Trollope, whose Domestic Manners of the Americans (1837) gives an interesting view of early-nineteenth-century life, was scandalized to see men and women enjoying the ocean together. She was calmed somewhat by learning that two ladies were expected to accompany each man to avoid a tête-à-tête immersion.

Not all the visitors found Cape May's simple pleasures to their liking. In 1825, one of them noted that time passed slowly and a number of his fellow lodgers were looking forward to the arrival of the steamboat that would take them home. Meanwhile, they did their best to occupy themselves:

Among our few amusements we swim, gather curious shells and pebbles upon the strand, walk the piazza and converse. A curious and laughable exercise is to try to walk blindfolded to any given object in a direct line. Ladies and gentlemen exercise at this. Some pitch quoits, some play dominos ... [and] last night one of the gentlemen played tunes on his flute and several made themselves merry with dancing in the dining hall.

For many, such a low-key daily routine is still the essence of a seaside vacation.

By 1840, Cape May had become the most popular seaside resort in the country. Yet it too had its rivals. Newport, Rhode Island, had a fashionable crowd and, with the opening of the Ocean House in 1846, a first-class hotel as well. The town of Nahant, on a peninsula off the Massachusetts North Shore—which was about as far from Boston as most Brahmins were willing to go—had its hotel and bowling alley. Nahant even had a sea-serpent—perhaps the first calculated publicity hoax in the country. The fearsome beast was first seen by one Marshall Price, who was later described as "nearsighted and at times somewhat passionate and enthusiastic—just the man to see a sea-serpent." The Boston papers fell for the hoax, and for several seasons the local presses turned out hundreds of sea-serpent affidavits from fishermen and the crews of coastal ships. Several expeditions were even fitted out to capture the beast; the most successful was led by a Captain Rich, who claimed to have harpooned the monster—only to have the big one get away. Eventually the excitement over the Nahant sea-serpent waned, but the American public has never tired of the succession of imaginative hoaxes and staged events that add a bit of zest to resort life.

Only Cape May was a serious rival for Saratoga. Although the town had followed Saratoga's model in the amusements it introduced, it could also offer the one thing its inland competitor could not: the sea, with its multiple attractions, not the least of which was

An artist's view of the joys of the seashore

a sure relief from the heat. A correspondent for the New York <u>Herald</u> captured the lure of beach life with these observations:

I tried to nap this morning about 11 o'clock, soon after my arrival, but my heavy eyelids were scarcely closed before I was startled with the merry shouts of a hundred voices, and looking out of my window, I was still more startled by the scene before me. I do not believe that Franconi's Hippodrome ever presents a gayer, more grotesque and animated scene than I witnessed. Hundreds of bathers, clad in garments of every shape and color—green, blue, orange, red and white—were gayly disporting before me, and within a few yards of my window. The blooming girl, the matronized yet blushing maiden, the dignified mamma, all were playing, dancing, romping, and shouting together, as if they were all of one age and were all alive with one feeling. I noticed several ladies of admirable shapes, whose forms Praxiteles might worship, most engagingly and fittingly clad, slowly promenading on the beach before they tempted the briny wave.

The good-natured rivalry between Saratoga and Cape May for the favors of the fashionable crowd occasioned some amusing incidents. Dr. John Clark, the owner of a bottling works at Saratoga's Congress Spring, refused to sell bottled Saratoga water to any of the sea resorts, claiming that it would give them too great an advantage. That problem was resolved by an enterprising hotel owner in Long Branch, also on the Jersey shore, who named a local mineral spring "The Congress."

Cape May had acquired its first luxurious hotel when Richard Ludlam built the Mansion House in 1832. All the older boardinghouses and hotels were subsequently enlarged, and several new buildings of architectural merit were added as investors realized that the popularity of the resort guaranteed a good profit.

Social life centered around the large hotels, which carried on a spirited rivalry to see which could provide the most successful attractions. Most of them had ten-pin bowling alleys, facilities for the popular sport of archery, and pistol ranges. Ice cream, once a rare treat, was now available in any number of ice-cream saloons. But the hotels put forth their grandest efforts in staging special events. In 1847, the Mansion House offered performances by the Virginia Serenaders and the opera <u>Stuffo</u> in its new entertainment hall. The Atlantic, now grandly rebuilt, put on a glittering subscription ball, while the Congress Hall gave an exhibition of fireworks on its broad lawn that lasted nearly an hour and a half. The greatest coup of the season, however, was the arrival of the popular Henry Clay at the Mansion House. The famed Southerner reportedly enjoyed sea bathing twice a day, but he lost a good deal of his hair to scissors-wielding, souvenir-hunting ladies.

Every hotel had a band, each conducted by a famous leader. Music was everywhere. The frequent hops and balls staged at one hotel or another were the mainstay of the social season. An observer marveled at the Congress Hall's new dining room,

The Mount Vernon as it was to have appeared when completed

the scene of many such balls:

Think of a hall 200 feet long, 45 feet wide, and 16 feet to the ceiling, without a pillar or post outside of its walls for a support. At night, when this hall is cleared of its tables and chairs, and hundreds of gas jets are brilliantly burning and flickering and the gay and elite are flushed with the giddy dance, then you behold a ball ...beautiful and fair.

Hotel porches offered opportunities for social gatherings, promenades, and a bit of strutting. They were equipped with comfortable chairs and card tables, and with pianos, touted as special instruments

most of which came from Vienna and had that peculiar tone which they caught from the damp sea-air which rusted the wire and softened the dampers and made the music sound like the blowing of the northeast wind through a girl's wet hair.

Fashion ruled here as at Saratoga. Ladies showed off their finery in beautifully appointed carriages that were promenaded along the town streets. Great pride was taken in the horses and rigs, and improved roads and the beach provided excellent driving conditions. Like Saratoga, Cape May had gambling clubs where the wealthy and famous could be seen trying their luck. The most popular gaming house was the Blue Pig, conveniently located right on the Congress Hall's lawn.

In the early 1850s, Cape May was thrust into the international spotlight by the building of what was then the world's largest resort hotel. Construction was begun on the Mount Vernon in 1852, and the hotel was opened to the public for the season of 1853. A description appeared in the London Illustrated News that summer:

The style is palatial; the dimensions far exceed those of any hotel in England. The building consists of a front four stories in height and 306 feet long and two wings extending backwards at right angles of similar height but each 506 feet in length. Enclosed between the wings is a large garden planted with beautiful shrubs and having in the middle a fountain of elegant design and elaborate construction. The garden is open at its southern extremity

to the sea, between which and the hotel itself a smooth and sloping sandy beach intervenes.

The writer apparently wrote his glowing account from press releases, for in 1853 only the front section of the building had been completed. By 1854, one of the wings had been added, allowing the hotel to accommodate 2,100 guests in rooms that were 9-1/2 feet square. In the middle of the front was a tower six stories tall, and the completed building was to have a five-story tower at the center of each wing and at the corners. These towers were an attempt to impose a larger architectural order upon the boxy façade with its continuous horizontal bands of verandas and balconies. Although the building was in the vaguely Italianate style which was then fashionable, its primary appeal was based on the novelty of sheer extent.

Another writer described the Mount Vernon's ornate and costly furnishings and then noted: "Among the luxuries of the place is that every bedroom has a bath attached, with hot and cold water always laid on"—this in a day when most guests counted themselves lucky to have a bath on their floor. Illumination was by gas manufactured on the premises, a luxury compared with the murk and smell of the oil lamps formerly used. The dining room, 60 feet wide and 425 long, was allegedly capable of seating 3,000 people, rather close together, at one time. The size and grandeur of the Mount Vernon were all the more amazing to the writer because Cape May was not a city—"just a quiet watering place."

The Mount Vernon was still unfinished when President Franklin Pierce came to Cape May for the summer of 1856. The resort was at its high point as a center of wealth and fashion. Then late that summer, the Mount Vernon caught fire. Within a few hours the vast wooden structure was reduced to smoking ashes. Later that year, the Mansion House too was destroyed by fire. It was a severe blow for the town, at a time when the first railroad to the shore had just been built to Absecon Beach, the future site of Atlantic City, and investment capital had shifted away from the older town to follow the crowds. The world of the resort hotel was indeed a fragile one.

Cape May did not decline overnight, though the tensions preceding the Civil War did keep many Southerners away. The outbreak of war, however, reduced Cape May to a ghost town. After the war, the construction of its own rail line led to a resurgence of the town's popularity. The Stockton House, built in 1868, was a first-class hotel on the model of Boston's Tremont House. Yet by this time the fashionable crowd had moved elsewhere. Cape May evolved into the quiet family resort that it is today.

CATSKILL MOUNTAIN HOUSE
New York

The resort hotel located to allow firsthand enjoyment of a recognized scenic attraction was the third type to make an early appearance in America. This country's first settlers had been blinded to the beauties of the natural landscape by their fear of it. Conversely, once nature began to be tamed, its wild state came to have a strong romantic appeal, especially to the city dweller. Americans began to see the wilderness, not as a wasteland, but as the unspoiled handiwork of God. It was only a short step from that attitude to the new awareness of beauty and a source of moral inspiration in natural scenery, which became fashionable in the early nineteenth century and has remained so to the present day. An increasing number of people sought out especially scenic places within easy reach that offered comfortable accommodations. By 1820, the scenic resort was firmly established.

The Catskill Mountains soon became popular with those who sailed past them on the Hudson River en route to Albany. Washington Irving recalled that on a voyage up the river as a boy, he had been fascinated by the mystery of the mountains and by the old Dutch folk tales associated with them. When travel literature became popular, the Catskills received endless praise. The view from majestic South Mountain was widely celebrated, especially after James Fenimore Cooper described it in The Pioneers:

"I have travelled the woods for fifty-three years, and have made them my home for more than forty," said Leatherstocking, "and I can say that I have met but one place that was more to my liking, and that was only to eye-sight, and not for hunting or fishing." "And where was that?" asked Edwards. "Where! why up on the Catskills...there's a place in them hills that I used to climb to when I wanted to see the carryings on of the world, that would well pay any man for a barked shin or a torn moccasin. You know the Catskills, lad; for you must have seen them on your left, as you followed the river up from York, looking as blue as a piece of clear sky, and holding the clouds on their tops, as the smoke curls over the head of an Indian chief at the council fire....the place I mean is next to the river, where one of the ridges juts out a little from the rest, and where the rocks fall, for

the best part of a thousand feet, so much up and down, that a man standing on their edges is fool enough to think he can jump from top to bottom." "What see you when you get there?" asked Edwards. "Creation," said Natty, dropping his rod into the water and sweeping one hand around him in a circle: "all creation, lad...if being the best part of a mile in the air, and having men's farms and houses at your feet, with rivers looking like ribbons and mountains bigger than the 'Vision', seeming to be haystacks of green grass under you, gives any satisfaction to a man, I can recommend the spot."

Even before The Pioneers appeared a group of local businessmen had decided to capitalize on the growing fame of the view from the mountain by building a hotel on the very brink of the precipice. A stock company was formed, and by 1823 the old road up the mountain face had been improved for stage travel and a small wooden guesthouse had been built. Aaron Burr was among those who visited that year. In 1824, H. G. Spafford's Gazetteer of New York reported "a superb hotel, of 60 by 24 feet, three stories, elegantly furnished and attended, erected by the 'Catskill Mountains Association', an incorporated company, with a capital of $10,000.00." The hotel quickly became popular, and only four years later one visitor noted:

The Pine Orchard is the resort of so much company during the pleasant seasons of the year, that the attractions of its scenery are redoubled by the presence of agreeable and refined society. Individuals of taste and leisure, and still more, parties of travellers, will thus often enjoy a gratification which is rarely to be found in a place naturally so wild and difficult of access.

While the cost of such a vacation was great, the benefits were clearly worth the price. Harriet Martineau recalled, during a visit in 1834:

A foreign tourist was heard to complain of the high charges! High charges! As if we were to be supplied for nothing on a perch where the wonder is if any but the ravens get fed! When I considered what a drawback it is in visiting mountain-tops that one is driven down again almost immediately by one's bodily wants, I was ready to thank the people devoutly for harboring us on any terms, so that we might think out our thoughts, and compose our emotions, and take our fill of that portion of our universal and eternal inheritance.

In 1839, the hotel was leased by Charles Beach, the energetic young stagecoach entrepreneur whose lines provided access to the mountaintop. Beach had made a small fortune providing passenger and mail service to the Hudson Valley. By the early 1840s, competition from the railroads and steamship lines put his stage lines out of business, but by that time Beach had bought the Mountain House. The hotel was then extensively remodeled, the dining room enlarged, and a kitchen wing added. The original building and lobby were brought up to the standards established by Boston's Tremont House. The Tremont was also influential as an example of the chaste, white, symmetrical beauty of the Greek Revival Style of architecture. In the late 1820s this style had become so strongly associated with American democratic ideals that its use for public structures was almost mandatory, and in commercial and domestic structures it conveyed equally powerful meanings. The stately new Corinthian colonnade applied to the front of the Mountain House was not only fashionable but seemed to impose an overall order upon the patched and lengthened façade. As a further patriotic gesture, the colonnade had thirteen columns, one for each of the original states in the Union. Behind the colonnade, the piecemeal construction was evident—in the parlor, for example:

There are eight windows, and not one of them opposite to any of the others; folding doors which have gone down the side of the room in some wild architectural dance, and have never returned; and a row of small columns stretching in an independent line across the room, quite irrespective of the middle. It is a dangerous parlor for a nervous man.

But most visitors found the Mountain House luxurious. Mrs. Elizabeth F. Lummis Ellet, a well-known critic, historian, and poet, visited the hotel around 1850 and was enthralled by its unexpected splendor:

It is spacious enough to accommodate a very large number of guests, having double and triple rows of goodly dormitories, all of a better size, and more comfortably furnished, than the sleeping-rooms usually appropriated to travellers at the fashionable watering-places. The drawing rooms are spacious, the principal one consisting of three large saloons opening into each other, or rather forming one. The dining hall is large enough for a feudal banqueting hall, its effect being increased by a range of pillars for the whole length down the centre, and these pillars are wreathed with evergreens, while between the numerous windows stand hemlock or cedar trees during the season, quite baronial in taste. As far as I know, this style of embellishment is unique; it is certainly very picturesque.

Beach took personal pride in affording his guests the luxuries and amusements offered by his flatland

A sketch by Thomas Nast of the Mountain House

competitors. Bathing facilities, a billiard hall, and a bowling alley were added. An extensive network of hiking and riding trails was established to notable outlooks and to nearby lakes and falls. The hotel even provided a minister for the devout. And the cuisine, according to Mrs. Ellet, was excellent:

Here is an almost wasteful profusion of strawberries, and other fruits of the season, freshly picked by the mountaineers, with cream and butter that does ample justice to the rich pasturage of this region.

Beach sought to own or control every facet of the service system on which his hotel depended. By 1840, the Mountain House had become, in the view of historian Roland Van Zandt,

a self-sufficient community: large gardens supplied fresh vegetables for the daily table; herds of cattle provided fresh dairy products; bakeries supplied pastry and bread. An exception was the daily supply of fresh meats: lacking modern means of refrigeration, the Mountain House had to import its meat from the distant village of Catskill. The meat was brought up early each morning while the guests of the hotel were still asleep. The wagons, horses, and even some of the roads were directly owned or controlled by the Mountain House itself.

The climate at the Mountain House, it was noted, was always ten to fifteen degrees cooler than in the lowlands. Malaria was unknown at that altitude. And of course, no other resort could match the advantages of the South Mountain site. As Bayard Taylor, the noted essayist and traveler, related in a letter to a friend in 1860:

We have front rooms at the Mountain House; have you ever had one? Through the white Corinthian pillars of the portico—pillars, which, I must say, are very well proportioned—you get much the same effects as through those of the Propylaea of the Athenian Acropolis. You can open your window, breathing the delicious mountain air in sleep (under a blanket), and, without lifting your head from the pillow, see the sun come up a hundred miles away.

The Civil War Years
WHITE SULPHUR SPRINGS
Virginia

All through the financially depressed 1840s, business at Virginia's springs lagged. By 1850, the return of prosperity again filled the cabins and taverns to overflowing. With old resorts jam-packed, new springs that had been little more than mudholes in a farmer's field a few years earlier were now being transformed into first-class watering places, complete with appropriate accommodations and a thick pile of physicians' reports testifying to the salubrious effects of the waters. Capon Springs even boasted a handsome brick hotel resembling those at Saratoga, with an elegant classical colonnade 35 feet high across the front.

At White Sulphur Springs, the construction of new cabins did little to relieve the congestion. One New England honeymooner reported that the parlors in the taverns were strewn with straw mattresses at night to accommodate guests without rooms. Clearly the time had come for the "Queen of the Southern Spas" to have a first-class hotel of her own. But financial mismanagement had put the resort heavily in debt. After attempting to solve their financial woes by forming a stock company, the springs' owners sold out to a group of Virginia gentlemen in 1857. For years, patrons of the resort had longed for it to be taken out of inefficient family management and run as a competitive business. The new owners built a cottage row, a bowling alley, and bathhouses, and most exciting of all, broke ground for a hotel some 400 feet long and 100 feet wide. The Grand Central Hotel—or the "White," as its patrons insisted on calling it—opened its doors in June 1858. At one end was a ballroom; at the other, a parlor "half again as large as the celebrated East Room" in the White House in Washington, D.C. In between there was a dining room that could seat 1,200 people with room to spare. The two floors above the main level contained 228 guest chambers, while the raised basement boasted a dark, cool bar, a restaurant, and offices. The kitchen, much to the irritation of the cooks, was "as dark as the Black Hole of Calcutta."

To the Southerners who frequented the springs, the hotel was a symbol of Southern enterprise and self-sufficiency. Even as the building was in construction, the North had been rocked by a severe financial panic that crippled its commerce. But the catastrophe had little effect on the agricultural South. While the North floundered, the South enjoyed a boom year. The Grand Central, built with Southern money and energy, seemed visible proof that the South had no need for the North at all.

Friction between Northerners and Southerners had increased sharply in the preceding years. Slaveholders found Northern resorts less and less hospitable. "Stay home," the Southern newspapers advised; "you are only insulted up there, you only pour your money into the pockets of the abolitionists who have sworn to destroy you." Drawing knives and pistols to defend the honor of the South and Southern womanhood grew so common that the newspapers tired of pointing out the obvious solution:

Why don't they visit the fine Southern resorts where the facilities, amusements, and the society, with its polished manner, courtesy, cleverness and propriety were equal, if not superior to any Northern spa?

That's just what Southerners began to do. The "White" experienced increasingly glittering seasons as the pressure for secession grew. In fact, a good deal of the pressure was focused at White Sulphur Springs. It was there that men like firebrand Edmund Ruffin chose to catch the wealthiest and most influential Southerners at their leisure and sway them to the secessionist cause. By 1860, the hotel had even installed a pistol gallery to allow young and old to polish up their marksmanship, while Edmund Ruffin grimly organized the ladies into shooting clubs. Even the children drilled on the lawns in front of the cottage rows.

When the Civil War broke out, the hotel saw rough service as a barracks and hospital for both sides. It only narrowly avoided the torch at the hands of the Union forces. The Civil War left the South in ruins,

Guests nicknamed the Grand Central Hotel the "White."

and with it the hotel that symbolized its aristocratic life. The resort buildings were in poor repair, and the furniture and hangings had been destroyed. Yet only two years after Appomattox, the hotel had been repaired and redecorated, and the new lessees expressed hopes for a modestly successful season. Slowly, the White's old patrons returned to recapture some of the glorious past and forget the humiliation of Reconstruction. With the arrival of General Robert E. Lee and a new generation of Southern belles in 1867, the stains of war seemed to have been washed clean. But a great deal of bitterness lay just below the surface. When General Lee sought to induce some of the young ladies to forget their animosity and do their part to heal the country's wounds by showing courtesy to Northern guests, only one would accompany him to be introduced.

The season of 1867 was a quiet one, but by 1868 the White seemed well on the way to recapturing its glittering past. Following Lee's lead, many of the most influential men in the South were in attendance —as were Northern political figures who courted their support. Resort life had returned to its brisk routine of horseback riding, excellent leisurely meals, and dancing. The ritual courtship of the belle was revived when the Billing, Wooing, and Cooing Society posted the gentlemanly rules of courtship in the main ballroom. The Southern public doted on the doings of belles like beautiful Mary Triplett or witty Mattie Ould. A newspaper correspondent reported:

Soft music floats on the air, and beauty haunts the bowers and groves. But if you will risk the loss of your senses, visit the magnificent ballroom, perhaps the finest in the world—"where youth and pleasure meet, to chase the glowing hours with flying feet." There you will behold every style of beauty in which our widespread country exults; the golden locks and azure eyes of the northern blonde, and the raven locks and black eyes of the southern brunette. But view them in motion, as "on gossamer pinions they float through the air" so buoyant, so sylph-like, that you do not realize that they are things of the earth, till, in the whirling mazes of the dance, you catch a glimpse of a foot and ankle.

Some towns even took up collections to send promising but underfinanced local belles to the White to make a good match.

By 1869, the railroad had reached White Sulphur Springs, firmly establishing its position as the premier Southern resort. More people came than ever before, and with them "enough tackle for a regiment." Belles could now bring all the gowns they wanted. It was common for them to wear one gown at breakfast, a second for the morning cotillion, a third for noontime dinner, a fourth for the afternoon concert, and a fifth for supper, the Treadmill—the evening promenade in the ballroom—and a night of dancing.

The season of 1869 was the climax of the golden age of the Virginia springs as many of the old stars of the South's great day gathered together for the last time at the White, the very symbol of Southern tradition. With the death of Robert E. Lee in 1870 and of other heroes in the succeeding years, the substance of this tradition gave way to myth.

SARATOGA SPRINGS

New York

In the years prior to the Civil War, Northern resorts had continued to prosper, despite the departure of most Southerners. While the outbreak of hostilities virtually closed down resorts that were near the front, Saratoga was safely removed from the conflict, and carefree vacation life went on almost as in normal times. In fact, in 1863 gambler and Tammany politician John Morrissey opened a race track there with such success that a second, larger track was built the following year. Although the war was far from the minds of the high-spirited crowds in attendance, it did have a profound effect on American life and attitudes and consequently on patterns of play and enjoyment that radically transformed the resort scene during the next decade.

The Civil War may have decimated and impoverished the South, but shrewd entrepreneurs of the North had taken advantage of the war to create vast new fortunes based on industry and profiteering. Not only were Northerners experiencing an unprecedented wave of prosperity and expansion, but the old values and constraints that kept in check the free expression of wealth had been severely shaken. Conspicuous consumption and the elaborate display of material success became the order of the day for the new rich of the industrial North; clothes became fancier, equipages showier, meals heavier and richer, decoration more and more elaborate, music brassier, rhetoric more pompous and flowery. One of the things newly rich Americans would have liked to buy was cultural roots on a grander scale than their own rather chaste colonial past provided. Americans were beginning to discover the grandeur and traditions of Europe through descriptive literature and direct personal experience. Home seemed rather dowdy and provincial by comparison. European culture seemed far better suited to the expression of wealth and sophistication than that of America.

The lives the new rich sought to lead also demanded appropriately opulent and cosmopolitan settings. The free-wheeling eclecticism of the period encouraged the incorporation of European and other more exotic motifs into richly decorative architecture and interior spaces. As always, resort hotels were quick to respond to the changing tastes of their patrons. The architecture of America's most cosmopolitan resort, Saratoga Springs, was among the best examples of Victorian eclecticism in the country.

Saratoga in the late 1860s was host to a diverse collection of tycoons, profiteers, socialites, sportsmen, and politicians. Bonanza kings and millionaire industrialists paraded before the public with an utter absence of self-consciousness. Here came colorful characters like the unscrupulous Jim Fisk, whose attempts to corner the gold market with his partner Jay Gould had precipitated the financial panic of Black Friday. Fisk enjoyed marching in gaudy uniform at the head of New York's Ninth National Guard Regiment; he owed his colonelship to his willingness to pay their bills and show them a good time. Here came "Coal Oil Johnny," the oil millionaire, who was determined to spend his wealth as quickly as it could accumulate. Here were the politicians of Washington and Tammany, and millionaire industrialists and sportsmen like William Henry Vanderbilt and William Travers. The young Henry James, writing for The Nation, observed of the men at Saratoga:

They suggest to my fancy the swarming vastness—the multifarious possibilities and activities—of our young civilization. They come from the uttermost ends of the Union—from San Francisco, from New Orleans, from Alaska. As they sit with their white hats tilted forward, and their chairs tilted back, and their feet tilted up, and their cigars and toothpicks forming various angles with these various lines, I seem to see on their faces a tacit reference to the affairs of a continent. They are

36

Above: Packing the trunks for Saratoga. Below: The much-enlarged Union Hall as it appeared in 1864

obviously persons of experience—of a somewhat narrow and monotonous experience certainly; an experience of which the diamonds and laces which their wives are exhibiting hard by are, perhaps, the most substantial and beautiful result; but at any rate, they have lived, in every fibre of the will.... They are not the mellow fruit of a society which has walked hand-in-hand with tradition and culture; they are hard nuts, which have grown and ripened as they could. When they talk among themselves, I seem to hear the cracking of the shells.

Here also came mothers intent on arranging a good match for their elegantly costumed and coiffed daughters. American and European fortune-hunters prowled for the golden opportunity. Saratoga was more than ever the haunt of social climbers and of the masses who came to see and be seen. In high season, the town took on the aspect of a nonstop cotillion or promenade. With the addition of the track, boat races, and John Morrissey's opulent red brick gambling casino, the summer seasons became more ostentatious year by year.

Saratoga's resort life was, as always, concentrated in its hotels. The most fashionable of the lot was the Union Hotel, Gideon Putnam's old Union Hall, which had been purchased by the Leland brothers in 1864 and once again greatly enlarged and modernized. The complex now boasted private cottage accommodations in addition to the regular room suites and an opera house and a church on the premises. The Union kept up a lively competition with its chief rival, the new brick and brownstone Congress Hall, built to replace the original Congress Hall, which had burned in 1866.

The rivalry was resolved when Alexander Turney Stewart, the Scottish-Irish immigrant who had made his fortune with New York City's largest department store, bought the Union in 1872 for $532,000, changed its name to the Grand Union, and spent another half-million dollars remodeling it into one of the largest and most lavish hotels in the world. Despite his wealth, Stewart's efforts to enter New York society had been futile. Perhaps he saw the ownership of the country's most celebrated resort hotel as an open door to social recognition. If so, he must have been disappointed, for Mrs. William Astor, the self-appointed guardian of New York's social elite, held that door firmly closed.

The Grand Union opened to the public in 1874. The five-story brick structure presented a 450-foot colonnaded and mansard-roofed façade to Broadway before folding back two wings, each nearly a quarter of a mile long, to enclose an elaborate elm-shaded garden. The hotel was a quantifier's dream, with over 1 mile of piazzas overlooking street and garden, 2 miles of corridors, 12 acres of flowered Brussels carpets, and 1 acre of marble in floors and table tops. The dining room could seat 1,400. The 824 spacious guest rooms and family suites were furnished with elaborately carved walnut pieces and thick lace curtains. Crystal chandeliers sparkled overhead in the public rooms. A steam-powered Otis elevator carried guests from floor to floor, thus making the previously hard-to-reach and undesirable top-floor rooms equal in price with those on the lower floors. People with the means could enjoy the privacy of a cottage suite.

Even the Grand Union soon felt competition. The United States Hotel, which had burned to the ground in 1865, was now rebuilt as a fit competitor for its neighbor. It too was a U-shaped, five-story brick mass fronting Broadway for 233 feet, with long wings extending back to enclose a 3-acre elm-shaded park. This hotel also boasted immense public rooms with superb appointments, 768 guest rooms, and a large number of cottage suites.

The cottage suite had originated in the 1820s when several of the larger hotels built cottages for overflow guests. Privacy, combined with the services and facilities of a luxury hotel, made the cottage an extremely popular option. Each suite contained a parlor and private bath in addition to several bedrooms. Meals could be brought in and carriages driven right to the door. The cottages also proved attractive to amorous couples. Saratoga had long felt pressure, from wealthy sporting bachelors and husbands whose wives and daughters were traveling elsewhere, to introduce lavishly appointed bordellos. Although the town fathers were concerned that the free-spenders might choose to patronize other, more obliging resorts, they remained firm in their refusal to allow large-scale prostitution at the springs. Prominent New York and Boston madams might bring their fairest women for display purposes, but a come-hither look and an address back home were all they were allowed to give. The hotels, too, took strong measures to keep ladies of the evening from prowling the lobbies and piazzas. Couples who gave the slightest hint of not being married were not admitted as guests, with the exception of certain big-spending regulars. The cottages, however, were free from restriction and surveillance. It was naively assumed that their high price would be insurance against rowdiness and indiscretion. Some wealthy indoor sportsmen allowed themselves to get carried away, stocking their apartments with a number of pretty young "nieces," "cousins," or "secretaries to help them keep up with office work," but by and large such cottage life was considered an acceptable compromise by the town fathers.

The immense crowds that swirled about Saratoga's hotels during the summer season presented an amazing spectacle of fashion and wealth. The concentration of such display in one tiny town was unprecedented and rather dazzling. Guests still dutifully made their way to the springs each morning, but the

Above: The new Grand Union Hotel
Center and below: The garden and
Broadway Piazza of the new United
States
Right: Taking the waters at Congress
Spring

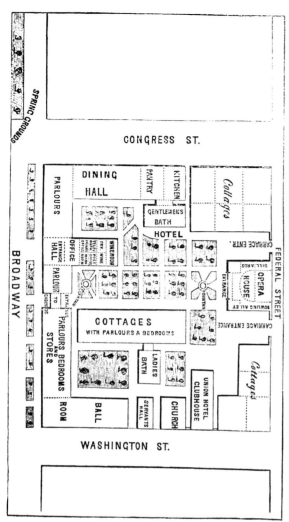

Left: The grounds of Union Hall in 1864. Right: The Grand Union dining room

attractions of fashion, gambling, and horse racing had for some time been the real raison d'être of the resort. Meals had grown in size and ceremony to the point where, in George Waller's words,

dinner was a challenge to longevity. There were eight courses of many choices—all bountiful and extravagant. It endured for two hours and after dinner the hotel was engulfed in contented lethargy.

The summer evenings were spent in seemingly endless hops, formal balls, and elaborate entertainments, while Saratoga's piazzas provided "front porch life without peer." Apart from the regulars, few of the spa's guests were prepared for the spectacle of

the vast verandas of the hotels, stretching as far as the eye could reach, or the spectacle of hundreds of people gossiping, reading, sipping fruit ices or watching the parade of passersby on Broadway while they rocked in the wicker rocking chairs and the diamonds they wore sparkled in the sunlight.

Even diamonds wouldn't necessarily gain one access to the elite of the United States Hotel's North Piazza. One had to possess a net worth of at least a million dollars to be welcomed by William Vanderbilt, Jay Gould, J. P. Morgan, or John D. Rockefeller as they planned financial maneuvers that would soon rock Wall Street.

LONG BRANCH

Saratoga's chief rival for the favors of the fashionable crowd at this time was Long Branch, on the New Jersey shore. Improved steamship and rail transportation now made it easily accessible from New York and other major cities of the Middle Atlantic States, and by 1860 the resort had become quite popular. Though the Civil War dampened the resort's gaiety, it quickly recovered and began to acquire a reputation as a favorite of prominent political figures and theatrical folk such as General Winfield Scott, Edwin Booth, and Maggie Mitchell.

It took more than a well-known clientele and an air of exclusivity to raise Long Branch to a resort of the first rank, for its rivals were formidable. The transformation was accomplished by the audacious scheme of attracting the most important and fashionable resorter in America: the President. Publisher George Childs and several of his friends, including George Pullman and financier Moses Taylor, presented President Ulysses S. Grant with an elaborate cottage in Long Branch. Grant was drawn to the resort by its reputation for gaming, riding, and driving, and he made the place his "summer capital." He found the whirl of social life trying, however, and after cutting a sorry figure at a ball given in his honor, was quoted as saying to his partner, "Madam, I had rather storm a fort than attempt another dance." To the great relief of its promoters, Grant's successors also took a liking to Long Branch and confirmed its reputation as the presidential resort.

Saratoga provided the model for Long Branch's development in many ways. The shore resort had the requisite gaming parlors and, with the construction of Monmouth Park in 1869, the first-class race track necessary to draw the wealthy sporting crowd and turf aristocracy. The last vestiges of the simple life were swept away as the new clientele demanded the best in accommodations, service, and entertainment.

The hotels grew in size and pretension. The elaborate Stick Style structures vied to monopolize as much of the edge of the sea bluff or, failing that, of the main street as they could. The Continental, for example, stretched 700 feet along the ocean and boasted a continuous piazza half a mile long.

Hotel rates averaged $4 a day, with four enormous meals included: breakfast at eight, dinner at two, tea at six, supper at nine. Each hotel had its own band for concerts and dancing, and during the afternoons, they played on the lawns of the hotels amidst shooting galleries and tents where soda pop and gingerbread were sold. On a typical day, two or three thousand people would swim at the beach below. The fashionable lady wore a bathing costume of "delicate rose flannel with pleatings of white, pink hose, straw shoes and a broad-brimmed hat of chipped straw tied with a pink flannel bow under the chin." The fashionable gentleman wore "a tight-fitting blue shirt with a white star on the breast or a loose sailor's shirt and trousers handsomely braided." The average person, however, merely rented a knit suit from one of the bathing concessionaires. On Ocean Avenue, vacationers paraded in victorias and landaus, exchanging the latest gossip and carefully observing each other's dress and paraphernalia.

It was said that everybody who was anybody sooner or later came to Long Branch. Indeed, a list of guests would read like a combination of the society, finance, and front pages of a New York or Philadelphia newspaper. Yet the very success of the place provided its undoing as an exclusive resort. It had a transitory air about it, lacking the solidarity and traditions of Saratoga or a growing cottage colony as at Newport. The beach, with its inherently more informal atmosphere, attracted "great throngs of cheap excursionists, small tradesmen and artisans with their families, with a sprinkling of roughs and sharpers—just such throngs as also go to Coney Island." Unlike Saratoga, Long Branch was unable to absorb the working-class vacationer who threatened to disrupt its carefully contrived atmosphere of exclusivity and high fashion. Long Branch became the resort of the common man.

Above: The elongated Mansion House. Below: The Iron Pier

Tourists at Mount Lowe above Pasadena, circa 1900

The Centennial to World War 1

The first golden age of the grand resort hotel was just one manifestation of the energy and self-awareness that characterized the American spirit from 1876 to the First World War. The Centennial Exhibition of 1876 in Philadelphia served as a prelude to this era by boosting national solidarity and stimulating further progress. Exhibits from each of the states gave visitors an idea of the vastness and variety of the nation and aroused interest in surveying the entire country at first hand. Easterners in particular were anxious to explore the mysterious lands of the Far West.

The period following the Centennial was one of tremendous expansion and mobility. It was an age of technological marvels, which seemed to promise a life free from toil. The electric light bulb, electric motor, typewriter, and a host of other new and curious inventions displayed at the Centennial Exhibition had become part of everyday life by the turn of the century. The linotype and multiple-printing press served America's growing passion for learning about the world in general and the habits, thoughts, lives, and dreams of fellow Americans in particular. High-quality illustrations, cartoons, photographs, and color printing gave the media a new impact and immediacy. The great differences of class, ethnic origin, religion, and living conditions in American life were made much more apparent.

The new industrial society of America created a great deal of new wealth for a few people. For those people, new money meant a new life-style. Simultaneously, this industrial society also possessed a new and much more complex social hierarchy, with many subtle distinctions between old and new money, vast and not-so-vast fortunes. To accommodate life at the top of the social ladder, the wealthy created a world of private clubs, societies, schools, residential developments, and organizations of all sorts, complete with elaborate settings and rules of behavior. The gigantic resort hotels that were built all over the country in this period were perhaps the most public part of this private world of the wealthy. These people, especially the new rich among them, were extremely competitive, at play as much as in business, and this competition and social one-upmanship clearly affected resort hotels. Undine Spragg, the ambitious heroine of Edith Wharton's Custom of the Country, overhears, to her obvious distress, a Washington socialite describe the Virginia resort she had considered the top of the social ladder as "this dreadful hole."

The modern grand resort hotel was created in this period through a symbiotic relationship between the new ease and the sheer excitement of railroad travel, and the newfound wanderlust of a class of Americans with both the leisure time and the money to indulge it. Rail lines spanned the continent in 1869, and during the following decades an extensive network of branch lines was built, enlarging the area through which Americans could travel in comfort. Obviously the American wilderness and the shore had been accessible for decades, but only to travelers with pioneering instincts, for the way was rough and often dangerous. The relative luxury of travel by train opened the entire continent to this new segment of the population, and particularly to the wealthy female. Although well-to-do Americans had enjoyed the comfort of private railroad cars since the 1870s, the appearance of the Pullman palace car around 1880 made first-class travel accommodations available to anyone who could pay the price. One traveler enthusiastically described his opulent surroundings:

The sleeping cars are fitted up with oiled walnut, carved and gilded, etched and stained plate glass, metal trappings heavily silver-plated, seats cushioned with thick

This New England inn exhibits the essential elements of a nineteenth-century resort: a wilderness setting, transportation, and the hotel itself.

plush, washstands of marble and walnut, damask curtains and massive mirrors in frames of gilded walnut. The floors are carpeted with the most costly Brussels and the roof beautifully frescoed in mosaics of gold, of emerald green, of crimson, sky blue, violet, drab and black.

The luxury trains also included library and lounge cars, as well as a dining car that offered a menu equaling those of Eastern restaurants. Indeed, the Pullman train was a hotel on wheels, and it served as an appropriate introduction to the resort that awaited its passengers at the end of the line.

Rail travel to the West and to Florida was at first quite expensive. It was estimated that a trip through the American West prior to the 1880s cost more than twice as much as a European tour. The cost was so prohibitive that as one Southern Californian put it, "it costs (tourists) too much to get here for the 'scum of the earth' to be among them." Occasionally, however, a price war would erupt, and in the 1880s at least one trainload of passengers traveled from Saint Louis to Los Angeles for one dollar per person.

Railroad and steamship companies encouraged travel on their own lines by organizing tours for people who preferred not to deal with the details of planning a long journey. The advent of the guided tour offered the assurance of comfort and respectable companionship. Private tour operators such as the

firm of Raymond and Whitcomb began to introduce the Pacific coast to groups of Eastern visitors in 1881. People could now view the scenic vestiges of the frontier in comfort. Schedules were even planned to take the tours through unattractive wastelands at night. Once on the Pacific coast, tourists were provided with first-class accommodations in resort hotels. Travel brochures and hotel advertisments from the late nineteenth and early twentieth centuries empha-size the proximity of lodgings to transportation, the uniqueness and often the sublimity of the surrounding scenery, and the luxury of the hotels themselves. As native Westerners were quick to point out, the East-erner's experience of the West was tempered by the conveniences of heat, artificial lighting, and frequently, gourmet cuisine. Hotel owners in the less-developed portions of the country took pride in providing all of the services available at contemporary urban hotels in the East, including elegantly manicured gardens — often in marked contrast to the natural landscape. The Hotel Raymond in Pasadena is a good example. It was built by Walter Raymond, whose father's tour groups provided a steady stream of dependable patrons. Constructed on a site donated by the Santa Fe Railway, it was a hotel such as might have been found in any Eastern city, except that here it was surrounded by lush gardens and orange groves. The staff met Eastern standards as well, for they worked the summer season in a Raymond hotel in the White Mountains of New Hampshire, coming out to Pasadena for the winter season.

Railroad owners had quickly discovered that they could double their investment by providing hotel accommodations both along and at the termini of their rail lines. Henry Morrison Flagler, for example, owned the Florida East Coast Railway and also a string of luxury hotels that dotted the east coast of Florida, from the Ponce de Leon in Saint Augustine in the north to a fishing camp on Long Key in the south. Thus, the traveler could stop at nearly any point in Florida and still be in the care of the Flagler organization. Hotels were often built not merely to stimulate tourist traffic but also as the centerpieces of new real estate developments. Hotels at Palm Beach, Florida, at Riverside and Coronado, California, and elsewhere were constructed by railroad and real estate interests to induce people to settle in those towns. The resort hotels of this period were both outposts of Eastern civilization and the seeds of future urban developments.

Sound management was essential to the smooth operation of a complex establishment like the resort hotel, and soon the structure and precision that typified the organization of other institutions were applied to hotels. In the new era of competition and expertise a resort hotel was simply too large an investment and too complex a business to be entrusted to amateurs. It was small wonder, hotel man Jesse Lynch Williams explained to his readers, that the manager of a great hotel received the same salary as a Supreme Court Justice. Clearly, the days of the hotel as a family enterprise were numbered.

Painters and writers of the early nineteenth century had already identified America's landscape as its most precious heritage, and after the Centennial, greater national self-awareness made the vast continental landscape a source of pride for all Americans. This period was the heyday of resorts in the Adirondacks, the Appalachians, the Midwest, and the mountains of New England. Travelers from the Midwest and the South began to frequent the shore towns of the Gulf States, and soon the winter vacation at Pass Christian, Ocean Springs, or Grand Isle became an established institution.

Although much of the North American continent already had been tamed by pioneers and frontiersmen, and by the railroad itself, travelers from the East fancied themselves explorers of a virgin land. Even today, one's first view of the Grand Canyon, Old Faithful, or Yosemite is a moment of personal discovery. For American tourists around the turn of the century, viewing the landscape was affected by notions of sublimity and exoticism. Steep riverside cliffs and irregular rock formations inspired lavish romantic and allegorical descriptions. As Louis Babcock said, mountains seemed to have the power to

bring man to a contemplation of his own littleness and the awful extent of infinite power. No man can behold the aspects of a nobly uplifted pinnacle or dome without realizing that his thought is expanded, unchained and newly gifted.

The landscape was often the raison d'être of a resort, and hotels were situated on or in view of noteworthy natural splendors. In the tradition of the Catskill Mountain House, many hotels perched precariously on the brink of deep canyons, high above dazzling waterfalls, or at the edge of picturesque woodland lakes. In some cases the natural landscape was accompanied by a man-made landscape as a reminder of Eastern civilization and amenity. At Mohonk Mountain House, for example, the Smiley family created both formal gardens and a seemingly natural, though in fact cultivated, wild mountainscape.

By the late nineteenth century, confrontation with nature for survival was largely a thing of the past, and amateur sportsmen now took to the wilds as a diversion. Several resorts in Maine promoted hunting excursions, which often resulted in huge kills. The sportsmen's wives were provided with tamer pastimes at the hotel while they waited for their brave woodsmen to return with the spoils. In Southern California, at the turn of the century, thanks to a vast and superb network of interurban rail lines, the use and enjoyment of the landscape became a pleasurable recreation. It was possible then (and is virtually impossible now) to throw snowballs atop Mount Lowe in the morning, enjoy a breathtaking ride down the mountainside for lunch in the orange groves of Pasadena, and conclude the afternoon with a dip in the surf of the Pacific Ocean. The American interest in wild nature had received official sanction in 1872, when Yellowstone Park was established as our first national park. The park system became the exemplar of the conservationist approach to landscape. But even here, concessionaires were permitted to build first-class hotel accommodations for those tourists whose appreciation of the wild did not extend to camping out or cooking over an open fire.

Resorts both at the seashore and at springs continued to be popular through the turn of the century as places where a healthy climate and mild recreation were the chief attractions. Health was still a popular excuse for getting away, although by the late nineteenth century a change of scene was valued as much for its benefit to one's mental state as to one's physical well-being. As Louis Babcock put it in the foreword to his resort travel guide of 1884:

As the human mind and body need sleep...so do they require each year a period during which they may escape from the noise and crowding of the city: from the toil

Above: The tourist train was a luxury hotel on wheels. Below: The costume of the familiar Harvey House waitress in 1890

and vexations of business, the wear and grind and routine of usual avocations and gain new vigor by simple contact with nature, breathing the air, using a healthful diet, seeing the sights.

The enthusiasm for outdoor sports that appeared after the Civil War assumed the proportions of a passion by the 1880s. Evening promenades were no longer sufficient exercise for the American population. Resort hotels all across the country sought to keep up with their patrons' interests by providing miles of hiking and riding trails, and facilities for canoeing, archery, golf, tennis, and polo. When the automobile appeared around 1900 as the newest sport for the wealthy, resorts added miles of good roads winding through scenic surroundings. The spectacular private road built for the guests of the Hotel Del Monte in Monterey, California, is now known to millions as Carmel's Seventeen Mile Drive.

By the time of the Centennial, resort hotels had generally grown in size and pretension. Their basic organization, however, had changed little. The arrangement of rooms along double-loaded corridors with the ground-floor space simply divided to form the public rooms continued to be the most efficient and economical type of plan. Long wings forming a U, a T, or an H still provided the maximum amount of light and air while also allowing easy access from the public spaces to verandas and gardens. With the introduction of the Queen Anne Style of architecture, architects began to experiment with modifications in the typical pattern.

The English Queen Anne Style was a contemporary revival and reinterpretation of forms from medieval and Elizabethan times used primarily for domestic buildings. While the style first appeared in England in the mid-1800s, the first American example of its use was Henry Hobson Richardson's Watts Sherman house of 1873. The shingle cladding, irregular plan, half-timbering, and leaded windows used in that house were to become the hallmarks of the Queen Anne Style in America. The American version of the style gained popular appeal as a result of the widely visited British pavilions at the Centennial Exhibition and quickly became the dominant picturesque style of the late nineteenth century.

American Queen Anne buildings were irregular in plan and massing. Sculptural forms such as gables, turrets, tall chimneys, dormers, towers, and pinnacles enlivened the façades and rooflines. The juxtaposition of stone, brick, clapboard, and shingles added textural variety to the building surfaces and enhanced the play of light across them. Broad porches, frequently with intricate stickwork and lattice, wrapped the base of the building, and smaller balconies were often cut into the roof. Soon some American architects began to look to the simple silver-shingled and gabled houses

of colonial New England for native inspiration. The result was the much more inventive Shingle Style, an architectural idiom that thrived in New England's cottage colonies during the early 1880s.

Throughout the nineteenth century, hotel architecture reflected contemporary fashions in residential design, and it was not long before the American Queen Anne and the related Shingle Style were adapted for resort use. Architects modified the typical hotel plan by introducing asymmetrical arrangements and irregular massing. Rooms were clustered to form large gabled pavilions, which sculpturally enlivened the façade. Although the addition of towers, dormers, and bays was often merely cosmetic, it did create interesting and eccentric interior spaces. Public spaces often opened into one another through broad arches, or were separated by see-through screens of wooden spindles; dark carved wood and richly colored wallpapers created an opulent atmosphere. In some hotels, most notably the Del Coronado, grand spaces of unusual shape became dominant features of the building. The American Queen Anne Style offered an exotic, picturesque, and adaptable architectural image in keeping with the wild, romantic landscapes then in vogue, whether mountainous, pastoral, or seaside.

Although the Queen Anne Style was introduced to America in the Northeast, hotel builders in the West and Midwest consciously adopted it to avoid the stigma of provincialism. Ironically, by the late 1880s many Eastern architects were looking to the palatial architecture of Europe for inspiration for very similar reasons.

When the Queen Anne Style began to fade from popularity, the picturesque informality it had embodied was given new expression in the Craftsman or Arts and Crafts Movement, which became popular after 1895. Although its sources lay in the English Arts and Crafts Movement and in the writings of William Morris, the architectural forms developed in America were quite different from English precedents. The movement was championed in this country by local arts and crafts societies and several popular periodicals, including Gustav Stickley's Craftsman magazine. Its proponents conceived of the good life as a blending of cosmopolitan tastes and liberal political sympathies with the traditional values of home and hearth. Craftsman architecture was marked by a deep respect for craftsmanship, a feeling for human scale, and a desire for harmony with nature. But because it also emphasized regional character, the movement did not promote a single architectural style. Buildings embodying the image of an English cottage, Bavarian lodge, Swiss chalet, log cabin, colonial cottage, or Southwest mission were all realized with a concern for fine workmanship and distinctive detailing, planning

BAR HARBOR
MT. DESERT ISLAND

Bar Harbor's large hotels were centers of social life.

suited to an informal lifestyle, a dramatic use of structure and materials, and often a studied air of rusticity. The most spectacular examples of hotels in these styles were built in the national parks of the West. This use of Craftsman imagery for resort buildings stemmed from a complex shift in attitude toward the landscape.

With the closing of the frontier, people began to appreciate the role of their old adversary, the wilderness, in forming the American character. Americans such as Theodore Roosevelt and the founders of the Boy Scouts sought to preserve the positive values of contact with the great outdoors through hiking, camping, woodcraft, and hunting. Unlike the Western resort builders of the 1880s, who tried to make their hotels appear as Eastern as possible, those of the early twentieth century sought empathy with the rugged wilderness.

The growing appreciation of the wilderness also generated public appreciation of its original inhabitants. Now that they were no longer a threat, Indians came to be viewed romantically as natural men fallen victim to an industrial society. By 1900, their value as a source of local color was recognized when the Santa Fe Railway began to use Indians in its advertising. The Spanish heritage of the Southwest had also been sentimentalized as early as 1884 with the publication of Helen Hunt Jackson's novel Ramona. At about the same time, Harvard-educated Los Angeles editor and author Charles Fletcher Lummis began his remarkable career as a one-man promotion bureau and spokesman for the Spanish and Indian Southwest. He and his followers provided Westerners with a respectable—though largely fabricated—romantic history, which in turn became the catalyst for so much of the Mission Style and the more flamboyant "Spanish" architecture in the Southwest, including the Mission Inn in Riverside and the Arlington and Santa Barbara Biltmore hotels in Santa Barbara, California.

One of the most significant supporters and popularizers of regional architecture was the Santa Fe Railway. Romantic Western themes began to appear in its advertising in the late 1890s. After the turn of the century, the railroad commissioned a number of stations and hotels designed in Mission or Pueblo architectural styles. For its hotels in the rugged Western national parks, it adopted rustic imagery drawn from the chalet, the hunting lodge, and the log cabin.

Although the vacationing public favored the picturesque styles, members of the architectural profession tended to regard them as interesting diversions and even as mere eclectic novelties. During the mid-1880s, when the popularity of the Queen Anne Style was at its height, many architects became uneasy with what they regarded as its arbitrary forms.

The Colonial Arms, Gloucester, Massachusetts

What was needed, they thought, was a return to solid fundamentals and timeless principles of beauty. For many, this search led to styles from the European past as representatives of venerable cultures. The path was shown by Richard Morris Hunt, the first American graduate of the École des Beaux-Arts in Paris. His erudite use of French forms for the homes of his wealthy New York patrons set new standards for formal, "correct" design and for professional competence. His designs were well suited to a generation of wealthy mansion builders who had viewed the glories of European architecture at first hand. Hunt's work and that of architects who followed his example were hailed as an American Renaissance and as sure evidence of America's cultural maturity. Classical academic design characterized by imposing grandeur was applied to many building types from houses and libraries to railroad stations and office buildings.

Resort buildings were also affected by this new architectural attitude. From 1890 on, hotels often resembled Italian palazzi, French châteaux, or other European models carefully chosen to harmonize with the character of the site. Hotels reminiscent of Renaissance palaces were built in the Rocky Mountains near the same rough-and-tumble mining camps where many of their patrons had made the fortunes that were being spent with such abandon. Hotels in California and Florida were designed to enhance the Mediterranean image and climate of those states. These buildings, so obviously palaces, were designed for a class of wealthy Americans in control of the emerging industrial nation in styles that reflected the extraordinary confidence of this era. And yet this rich architectural eclecticism of the turn of the century also provided a sense of cultural assurance for a nation somewhat unsettled about the meaning of its roots.

The Grand View Hotel in the Grand Canyon sits atop its main attraction.

MOHONK MOUNTAIN HOUSE
New Paltz, New York

The best and most familiar view of the Mohonk Mountain House is from the hiking trails across the beautiful mountaintop lake from the hotel itself. From there, the building seems to grow from the rocks like a craggy medieval castle that time forgot—a world apart from the bustle of the New York State Thruway just a few miles distant and a few thousand feet below.

Albert K. Smiley, a Quaker schoolmaster from Providence, was introduced to the Shawangunk Mountains by his twin brother Alfred in 1869. He was so impressed by the beauty of Mohonk Mountain and its lake that he borrowed every cent he could to acquire a small tavern-guesthouse perched at the water's edge. Smiley's intention was to operate the tiny resort for the pleasure of his family and friends. The place proved so popular that the building had to be enlarged to accommodate 40 people, the first in a long chain of additions. The oldest extant part of the present structure was completed in 1879. Architects Napoleon Le Brun and James E. Ware both made major additions, the last of which was completed in 1901. The result is a rather motley but pleasing collection of styles and materials with charming towers, balconies and odd roofs creating the impression that it has grown on the spot like some piece of architectural coral. The building is far more impressive as an object in the landscape than are any of its parts or its interiors. Indeed, the additive construction makes finding one's way around inside somewhat confusing.

The two parts that do stand out are the Stone Building, which occupies the center of the composition, and the adjacent Parlor Wing, both designed by James Ware. Built of rusticated stone and articulated by towers, turrets, and a forest of chimney stacks, the former is the most fortresslike section of the hotel. In contrast to the massive stonework, the guest-room balconies resemble a construction scaffold or a mass of summer gazebos stacked one on top of another.

Between the Stone Building and the lake is the Parlor Wing, an airy, chaletlike structure which contains a single large lounge and public porches overhanging the water, supported by steel trusses. It is this part of the hotel, sitting almost on the site of the original tavern, that remains in one's memory. It calls to mind an es-

The Stone Building (left) and the chalet-like Parlor Wing (right) of the Mohonk Mountain House

pecially large summerhouse, more spacious and refined than but similar to the tiny gazebos and rustic lean-tos that dot the hiking trails atop the rocky bluffs on the far side of the lake. The long rough building behind the parlor acts as a buffer against the parking lot, the road down the hill, and the real world beyond.

The sense of splendid isolation, retreat, and regeneration through healthy exercise and the enjoyment of nature has always been an important part of the Mohonk experience. The Smiley family's Quaker faith and interests made the hotel a center for conferences on world peace, education, and Indian affairs. Mohonk was also a temperance house until recently, when some of the rules were relaxed. Still, much of the original emphasis on vigorous outdoor life remains.

His interest in landscape design and the preservation of Mohonk's natural charms led Albert Smiley to acquire over 5,000 acres of land adjacent to the hotel. Imported soil and great determination converted acres of rocky ground into the beautiful flower gardens that are still one of Mohonk's principal attractions. In addition, miles of hiking trails and a vast system of carefully constructed carriage roads make the pleasures of the forest available even to the hotel's more sedentary guests. Automobiles were not allowed to disturb Mohonk's quietude until 1930, and even today their encroachment on this beautiful place is kept to a minimum. The day visitors that come to enjoy the trails and the lake often hike in from the stone gate, several miles down the mountain.

The Mohonk Mountain House as seen from the lookout tower across the lake

POLAND SPRING HOUSE
Poland Spring, Maine

The Poland Spring House was also a family affair. The Ricker family migrated from Saxony to New Hampshire in the mid-seventeenth century, settling in the foothills of the White Mountains about 25 miles north of Portland, Maine, in the town now known as Poland. Their property lay along the stage route from Portland to Montreal. In 1797, Jabez Ricker opened an inn for travelers.

A number of legends have grown up around the discovery of the healing powers of Poland Spring water. The spring had been ignored for several generations as little more than a swampy spot in the Ricker cow pasture. It is not clear whether it was the beneficial effects on the neighbor's ox or on Jabez's grandson Hiram that inspired that young man to spread abroad the virtues of Poland Spring water in the 1850s. In any case. Hiram had found his calling.

Samples of Poland Spring water were sent to physicians around the country, and in 1859 Eliphalet Clark of Portland was the first doctor to endorse it for the treatment of kidney and liver diseases. Once the medicinal value of the water was established, the Rickers began to bottle and sell it through distributors in every major American city. Poland Spring water was even available in Saratoga. The fame of the spring attracted an ever-increasing number of visitors to the old inn, and several additions to the structure were made.

In 1875, Hiram Ricker decided to build a larger and grander hotel, and a year later the Poland Spring House opened with its 300 rooms booked in advance. Later additions increased the capacity of the hotel to 600. The plan consisted of two wings at right angles to one another joined by a square tower, the visual focus of the façade. An observation room at the top of the tower afforded a panoramic view through huge windows. Turrets punctuated the center and ends of the wings. In 1881, John Calvin Stevens and Albert Winslow Cobb made additions in the currently fashionable Queen Anne Style. Their dining room featured the largest piece of glass in the state of Maine. The hotel continued to be modified and elaborated. In 1903, architect Harry Wilkerson even brought the Beaux-Arts Movement to bear by topping the main tower and an adjacent turret with domes. The picturesque bays and verandas admitted as much light and air as possible as well as lending variety to the long primary façades.

The Poland Spring House as it appeared around 1890

Rooms on the favored outer walls of the L-shaped ground plan were generally larger and equipped with private baths. The existence of more and less desirable rooms in the hotel was reflected in a similar hierarchy in the dining room, where one's stature among fellow guests was indicated by placement at a particular table. Luxury hotels have always made an asset of snob appeal and restrictions, and during the late nineteenth century the Poland Spring House was hardly alone in vicious discriminatory practices banning Jews, blacks, Catholics, Irish, and Italians. Ironically, Irish, Italians, and German Catholics made up most of the extensive staff of servants who not only prepared the meals and maintained the building but also operated the water-bottling plant and the dairy and vegetable farms that supplied the hotel.

The Poland Spring House continued to grow in size and in popularity through the turn of the century and was able to survive as an exclusive hotel through World War I. As the twentieth century progressed, however, changes in vacation patterns diminished the number of people who returned year after year to spend the entire season. The Ricker family finally sold the property in 1940. During the 1950s, various corporations tried to revive the hotel with little success. A Job Corps training center occupied the building from 1967 to 1970 and made numerous ill-considered alterations. In 1972, a new owner began making plans to restore the Poland Spring House and open it as a resort once again, but a fire on the evening of July 3, 1975, consumed the entire hotel.

WENTWORTH-BY-THE-SEA

Portsmouth, New Hampshire

The first Wentworth, which opened in 1870, was a simple, boxlike clapboard building of 90 rooms crowning a beautiful island near Portsmouth. By 1879, a new owner had built another story, with a fashionable mansard roof and an elaborate stick-work piazza—the first of the many additions that can be clearly seen in the façade. The hotel enjoyed great popularity, and in 1911 it served as the setting for the Russo-Japanese peace conference intended to end conflict in Asia. The fanciful boat-shaped pool house and salt-water pool were added during the 1920s. At the same time, much of the Victorian woodwork was removed to give the complex a more up-to-date appearance. Fortunately, much of the Wentworth's late-nineteenth-century atmosphere remains with no sacrifice of twentieth-century comfort.

THE BALSAMS
Dixwell Notch, New Hampshire

The Balsams has outlived most of its mid-nineteenth-century contemporaries through careful restoration and innovative management. In addition to all the entertainment and sports facilities of a major resort, its winterized buildings and its own ski area allow the hotel to operate the year round. Its lumber needs and supplementary income are provided by a sawmill on the property and by 15,000 acres of carefully managed forests. The scrap from the logging operation and the hotel's combustible garbage are burned to provide all its heat and electricity.

CONEY ISLAND

New York

Long Island's first settlers considered the expanse of sand dunes along Coney Island's Atlantic shore to be of little value. In 1829, in the hope of stirring up some business, the Gravesend and Coney Island Railroad and Bridge Company built the Coney Island Hotel and a causeway to provide easy access to it. However, things at the future resort remained slow.

In the 1840s, "Commodore" Cornelius Vanderbilt entertained similar ambitions when he built the Oceanic Hotel as the terminus of his coach and steamship lines. Two fires put an end to this venture, leaving the beach to New York's toughest elements, who had begun to gather in the cheap hotels, brothels, saloons, and gambling dens that occupied the beach's west end. Coney Island soon developed quite an unsavory reputation.

However, the demand for a first-class seaside resort within easy reach of New York City was strong. Banker August Corbin saw the potential of the place when he used the old Coney Island Hotel as a retreat for his invalid wife that was also within commuting distance of New York. With his financial backing, the New York and Manhattan Beach Railway built the Manhattan Beach Hotel in 1877. Architect J. Pickering Putnam assembled several large rectangular wooden pavilions on hundreds of piles sunk in the sand, to form a picturesque, irregular Queen Anne mass. The original building contained about 150 guest rooms and an open-air dining room that could also be used by nonguests, provided they brought their own food. Verandas were located to take advantage of the cool sea breezes, while to the rear a train shed extended to the nearby tracks. The Manhattan Beach Hotel proved an immediate success and was enlarged several times by the addition of several towered wings and auxiliary pavilions including a covered amphitheater.

Almost immediately, other first-class luxury hotels were built nearby. The Brighton Beach Hotel, with creamy white walls and red roofs and trim, opened in 1878. The fabulous Oriental Hotel, sporting corner pavilions and exotic decoration, opened the following year, catering to wealthy full-season guests rather than to transients. All three hotels spent money lavishly to draw crowds of respectable citizens. The residents of Coney's disreputable west end were held at bay by undemocratic but

The popular image of Coney Island in the 1930s: Luna Park by night, with thousands of lights outlining architectural details

MANHATTAN BEACH HOTEL.

J. PICKERING PUTNAM, ARCHITECT, BOSTON.

effective wire fences. Admission to the better beach cost a nickel. Visitors were entertained by balloon ascensions and plays. Bands played on the hotel lawns and on the fashionable iron pier where one might lunch on clams while enjoying the music of Patrick Gilmore or John Philip Sousa. Prize fights and dances added zest, while the ever popular attraction of sea bathing was enhanced by night illumination from arc lamps. The most spectacular entertainment was James C. Paine's fireworks, depicting "The Last Days of Pompeii," "The Burning of Rome," and other nightly conflagrations. By the early 1880s, for aristocrat and common man alike, no trip to New York was complete without a visit to Coney Island.

Gradually, the flavor of Coney changed as cheaper, thrill-oriented amusements and side shows proliferated. By the mid-1890s, the aristocracy had moved elsewhere and Coney Island had become a playground for the masses. The tamer entertainments of the old hotels had been surpassed by the illuminated marvels of Dreamland and Luna Park. The original attractions of sun and sea were gradually superseded by bright lights, fast rides, and foot-long hot dogs as the components of Sunday escapism.

Left, above: The Manhattan Beach Hotel
Left, below: Paine's fireworks depicting the last days of Pompeii
Above: The elaborate Oriental Hotel

GRAND HOTEL
Mackinac Island, Michigan

Mackinac Island has attracted tourists since the Civil War. Today it retains much of its nineteenth-century character, in part because automobiles are banned. Its location in the Straits of Mackinac, which joins Lakes Michigan and Huron and separates the Upper and Lower Peninsulas of Michigan, made Mackinac Island an important part of a resort circuit that included Petoskey, Traverse City, Saint Ignace, Les Cheneaux Islands, and Sault Sainte Marie. Steamers and trains alike brought tourists through the Great Lakes region to enjoy the splendid scenery and fine resorts like the Grand Hotel.

An eighteenth-century fort and battleground, wooded trails, and private cottages make up the backyard of the Grand, which sits majestically on a hill above the Straits of Mackinac. But it is the front of the hotel, overlooking the Straits, which looms large in the memories of visitors. The Grand Hotel boasts of having the longest front porch in the world—880 feet, or one-sixth of a mile. It stretches the entire length of the façade and is punctuated at each end by a semicircular bay. Elongated Tuscan columns on pedestals rise four stories to support a fifth-story addition, which serves visually as a weighty entablature. The sunbathed porch is complemented, and indeed challenged for importance, by a vast manicured lawn densely inhabited by outdoor furniture.

The use of the colonnade gives unity and grandeur to what would otherwise be a fairly undistinguished wooden box. This reserved, even austere façade is unlike those of the more exuberant Queen Anne Style typical of its period. It recalls instead the Greek Revival Style, with its reminders of ancient civilizations and of democratic visions of America. The Grand is an elegant successor to the Greek Revival hotels of the 1830s and 1840s.

In 1882, Senator Francis B. Stockbridge of Michigan purchased the site on Mackinac Island with the intention of building a "grand" hotel, and in 1887, the original building, only half the size of the current one, was constructed. John Oliver Plank leased and managed it until 1890. Additions in 1897, 1912, and 1919 enlarged the building to its present size. The Michigan Central Railroad, the Grand Rapids and

Horses and bicycles provide transportation on Mackinac Island, shown here on the main approach to the hotel.

Indiana Railroad, and the Detroit and Cleveland Navigation Company made up the stock company for the Grand Hotel, and "Commodore" Cornelius Vanderbilt was its first president. Thus, the Grand had a typically intimate connection with the transportation systems that serviced it. During its original short season of July and August, it hosted the first families of Chicago, Saint Louis, and other Midwestern cities. Cyrus G. Luce established the tradition that made the Grand Hotel the unofficial summer headquarters of Michigan's governors.

Noteworthy guests have included Presidents Grover Cleveland, William Howard Taft, Franklin D. Roosevelt, and of course Theodore Roosevelt, as well as Marshall Field, Mark Twain, and William Astor. In 1946, the Grand achieved celluloid immortality as the setting for the movie This Time for Keeps, in which Esther Williams performed one of her unforgettable fantasy water-ballet sequences in the hotel's serpentine pool. The frequent marriage of hotel setting and movie set suggests the appeal of illusion and make-believe that both the hotel and the movies hold for the American imagination.

Despite its fame, the Grand was a financial burden to its operators through the first four decades of its history. In the 1890s, a severe depression added to the difficulty of maintaining a hotel on this scale, especially when it produced income for only two months out of the year. Its relative isolation made provisions and services not only difficult to obtain but also very expensive. Well into the twentieth century, its managers were unable to operate in the black, and the Depression of the 1930s put the Grand in an especially precarious position. Although conditions had not improved by the time of the Second World War, owner Stewart Woodfill was determined that the hotel would remain open despite a shortage of both employees and guests. In the summer of 1942, the formal dining room was transformed into a cafeteria because only six waiters could be found. Since the war, however, the Grand has enjoyed prosperity under an expanded six-month season, catering to both conventions and family groups.

Today as always, hotel guests arrive by boat from Mackinaw City and are met at the ferry dock by a horse-drawn carriage, which takes them to the door of the hotel lobby. This slow-paced, gracious arrival is the perfect introduction to the relaxed atmosphere of the Grand Hotel.

The Grand Hotel boasts the longest front porch in the world.

GROVE PARK INN

Businessman E. W. Grove of Saint Louis was a patent-medicine king. Grove's Tasteless Chill Tonic and Bromo-Quinine Laxative made him a fortune, but he was unable to devise a remedy for his own bronchial ailment. Only the cool, clean air of Asheville seemed to help.

Asheville had begun to attract health-seekers and sufferers from tuberculosis in the years just following the Civil War. With the coming of the railroad in 1881, Colonel Frank Cox realized that the area would draw crowds if first-class accommodations were provided. He subsequently bought a beautiful hill on the edge of town and erected a gigantic wooden Queen Anne Style hotel. The Battery Park, as it was called, opened in 1886. Colonel Cox had been right in his estimation of the place: his hotel not only became the social center of the region but attracted the famous, wealthy, and powerful from both North and South. George Washington Vanderbilt fell in love with Asheville when he came down during the season of 1887. He soon began to acquire the vast holdings of land that became his famous "Biltmore" estate.

The presence of one of America's richest men acted as a stamp of approval for the region and a catalyst for further growth. New hotels were constructed, the most notable of which was the Kenilworth of 1891. Its architects, Price and Price, broke away from the typical long-winged hotel form by adapting the image of a Scottish baronial castle to the highlands of North Carolina. The building had rooms tightly grouped around a high central lobby.

Concern for their health continued to bring visitors to the resort during the prosperous 1890s, though the decline of the tubercular pallor from fashion and the growing awareness of the dangers of the disease led the major hotels to refuse lodging and service to consumptives. Healthy outdoor sports in the pure, malaria-free air became the town's primary attraction.

E. W. Grove visited Asheville at this time, and took a liking to the town. He purchased large tracts of land near the Asheville Country Club, where he laid out an exclusive subdivision. Then he bought the western slope of adjacent Sunset Mountain with the intention of building a hotel. Intrigued by the idea, Grove's son-

The Grove Park Inn, as seen from the golf course, resembles an archetypical rustic cottage.

in-law, newspaper editor F. G. Seeley, decided to design the building and act as its contractor himself. The rustic simplicity of the
Craftsman Style of architecture, then at the height of its popularity,
obviously had a great appeal for him. So too did the host of well-
publicized experiments with fireproof construction using reinforced
concrete. The building Seeley designed had four sections, each
with exterior walls of reinforced concrete faced with gigantic
boulders hauled in from South Mountain, some of them weighing
over three tons. These walls were 4-1/2 feet thick at the base.
The interior walls were formed of a double layer of 3-inch hollow
concrete blocks with an air space between, which made them
nearly soundproof. They were then plastered and covered with an
oak wainscot 5-1/2 feet high. The floors were of reinforced concrete, as was the roof, with its drooping curves covered with red
ceramic tiles intended to recall thatch. Great attention was given to
practical details and conveniences. Water, steam, and electric lines
were placed out of sight in conduits in the walls, and radiators

Above: The rugged lobby
Right, above: The hotel under construction
Right, below: A tastefully furnished guest room

were hidden from view. Not one bare electric light bulb could be seen; lighting was all indirect.

The interior furnishings were handmade pieces in the Craftsman Style, as were the copper chandeliers and lamps, all manufactured by Elbert Hubbard's Roycrofters of East Aurora, New York. Apparently the rustic simplicity of Grove Park Inn caused some guests, used to the applied decoration of other hotels, to fear that things were not first-rate. The management did its best to dispel such apprehensions with statements like the following:

Grove Park Inn is unlike any other hotel in the world and is as different in spirit and management as the building is in character. There is nothing fancy about the building or its furniture. But there is a plain, rugged honesty mingled with a quiet atmosphere of charm, that brings from visitors the universal expression. "It's so restful!" There isn't a piece of veneered furniture in the Inn. There isn't a figured rug—nor a fancy counterpane. There isn't a piece of wall paper anywhere, nor is there a figure or a flower on any of the 12,000 pieces of linen. But the furniture is of the finest solid Indiana quartered white oak, finished by hand, and even the three thousand drawer handles were made by hand by the Roycrofters from solid copper. Every drawer has a latch that makes it impossible to pull it out and let it fall on your foot.

The French rugs get their beauty from their matchless quality rather than from fancy designs. Instead of wall paper the bedroom walls are covered with the finest quality of prepared burlap in soft pastel shades, and this same spirit of simple elegance runs through every detail on the Inn from the hammered silver on the tables to the mammouth boulder fireplaces in the "Big Room." The management is in keeping with the building—home-like and sincere—and the guests who have enjoyed the Inn say it is like a "big old-fashioned home." This is what we have tried to make it. We feel that we have succeeded.

The Inn may have been like a "big old-fashioned home," but it also offered every luxury and sports facility expected of a grand resort hotel. From the time of its opening in 1913, it quickly became Asheville's most popular hotel, attracting the likes of Thomas Edison, Harvey Firestone, Woodrow Wilson, and Henry Ford. A few years later F. Scott Fitzgerald worked here while consuming amazing quantities of beer.

Throughout its early years, Grove Park Inn refused to allow conventions to use the building, feeling that this would damage the relaxing atmosphere. With the financial difficulties of the Depression years, however, that policy was modified and later abandoned. A few years ago the Inn was purchased by the Del Webb Corporation and extensively remodeled and refurnished to cater to the convention trade. Although much of its interior charm has now been compromised by paint, acoustical tile, modern furniture, and wall-to-wall carpeting, the building still retains much of its original exterior character.

The Scottish baronial Kenilworth by Price and Price was thought appropriate in character for the highlands of North Carolina.

317. KENILWORTH INN, ASHEVILLE, N.C.　　　　　　　　　　　　　　　COPYRIGHT 189

THE PONCE DE LEON & THE ALCAZAR

Saint Augustine, Florida

The growing popularity of the winter vacation brought tourists to Florida in ever-increasing numbers during the 1880s. Jacksonville offered a temperate climate and the convenience of a Northern city, while nearby "everglades, swamps and strange rivers bordered by luxuriant vegetation (gave) one an impression of the freaks of nature run wild." Of course, the guidebooks that described the mysterious cypress swamps and fearsome alligator hunts were also quick to assure the would-be adventurer that everything was quite safe.

Saint Augustine, the oldest European settlement in the continental United States, also offered a romantic past that suggested

the Middle Ages and the time when Spanish cavaliers ventured across the great deep in search of Eldorado and the Fountain of Youth. . . . it is as if some little dead-alive Spanish town with its fort and gateway and Moorish bell towers had broken loose, floated over here and got stranded on a sand bank.

And best of all, English was the language spoken.

Standard Oil millionaire Henry Morrison Flagler and his wife were among the many well-to-do Americans attracted to Saint Augustine. Flagler took a liking to the quaint little town, and after conferring with the manager and builder of Saint Augustine's one modern hotel as well as with several leading citizens, he decided to erect a luxury hostelry of his own. The Ponce de Leon, named for the Spanish discoverer of Florida, would be a Spanish palace — in concrete. For his architects, the millionaire chose John M. Carrère and Thomas Hastings, two talented young graduates of the École des Beaux-Arts in Paris who as yet had no major achievements to their credit. Flagler was no doubt influenced by his long friendship with Hastings' father, who was his family minister. Still, the choice was an excellent one, for the young men recognized the chance to make their reputations and worked tirelessly to produce a great building.

Construction began during the summer of 1885. The marshy site was filled with sand, and hundreds of pine pilings were driven to support the foundations. Then the slip-formed walls of cement, sand, and pearly coquina-shell gravel began to rise, with a limited use of iron reinforcing. The Ponce de Leon was the first large cast-

The main gate to the entrance court of the Ponce de Leon Hotel helps to establish the hotel's architectural character.

concrete building in this country. It had other modern features as well, including four Edison dynamos in the boiler plant to provide electricity for several thousand lights—one of the first such lighting systems in the world. The hotel's water was pumped from deep artesian wells to large tanks in the building's twin towers. Oddly enough, the architects saw no need for private bathrooms, and these had to be added later.

As the four-story Spanish Renaissance structure neared completion, an army of craftsmen began to decorate the building under the direction of Carrère and Hastings' brilliant young designer, Bernard Maybeck. Fanciful historical symbolism ran rampant. Representations of the Lion of Leon, the symbol of Juan Ponce de Leon, ornamented gateposts and held light bulbs clenched in their teeth in the rotunda and dining room. Dolphins alluded to the nearby River of Dolphin. Even the doorknobs were modeled after sea shells.

Inside the front gate lay a 10,000-square-foot garden court surrounded by vine-covered verandas and filled with splashing fountains and exotic plants. Beyond that, the archway of the main entrance led to the rotunda at the very heart of the building. This vast space, over 80 feet in height, had a great dome supported by four tiers of oak pillars carved to represent the elements and the muses. Rich mosaics covered the floor, and allegorical paintings by George Maynard representing Adventure, Discovery, Conquest, and Civilization graced the dome. To the right of the rotunda lay the offices and parlors; to the left, the stately ballroom

Above: The Ponce de Leon employed Spanish Renaissance styling, which was felt suitable to the character of old Saint Augustine. Right: The magnificent rotunda with its marble mosaics, carved oak, and frescoes

The swimming pool in the Alcazar Casino

with its Tiffany chandeliers, carved wood paneling from New York, and painted ceiling by Virgilio Tojetti imported from Paris.

Behind the rotunda and up a flight of polished marble stairs lay the magnificent dining room. It was square, with semicircular apses, and could seat 700 people. Circular musicians' balconies overlooked the room; Tiffany stained glass gleamed in the clerestory windows. The ceiling was decorated with Maynard's representations of the four seasons and a pictographic history of Florida. Although the public rooms were the most elaborately decorated spaces of the Ponce de Leon, every one of the hotel's 450 guest suites and the host of private parlors and reading, game, and lounge rooms were also luxuriously furnished. The draperies, carpets, and carved rosewood, walnut, and mahogany furniture were said to have cost $1,000 per room.

Flagler did what he could to assure the success of his new hotel. Not only did he send out hundreds of promotional books to the clientele he hoped to attract, but he also purchased and improved the rail line serving Saint Augustine, renaming it the Florida East Coast Railway. Not all Flagler's friends thought the investment sound or sensible. "Why risk so much money in Florida?" they asked. "For about fourteen or fifteen years, I have devoted my time exclusively to business," came the reply, "and now I am pleasing myself."

Even Flagler had not fully understood, when he started, the extent to which his financial commitment to Saint Augustine would grow. Long before the Ponce de Leon was finished he realized that amusements for his guests and more moderately priced accommodations would have to be provided. Carrère and Hastings prepared designs for the Casino and for the Alcazar hotel, which were built across the street from the Ponce de Leon. The Casino contained a large indoor swimming pool, therapeutic baths, a billiard room, a bowling alley, and a ballroom. Tennis courts and later a golf course were located nearby; the moat of the Castillo de San Marcos, the oldest Spanish fortress in North America, provided a formidable water trap. The Alcazar was a concrete structure like the Ponce de Leon, but with a distinctive Moorish character. Shopping arcades surrounded its interior garden court and an elaborate terrace crowned the roof. From the first, the Alcazar proved to be an extremely popular place. Eventually a lobby and dining room were added to allow it to operate independently of the Ponce de Leon.

Provisions were made to house the hotel's small army of skilled workers in a wing over the kitchen behind the Ponce de Leon's dining room. Chefs, waiters, musicians, guards, and the main-

One of the Ponce de Leon's elegant public rooms

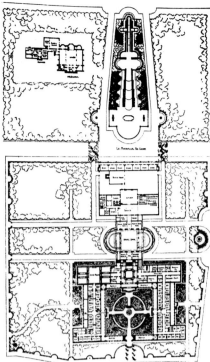

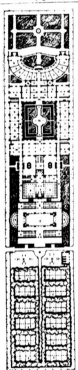

tenance staff were career hotel workers who worked at Northern resorts during the summer months and then came South for the winter. Black employees were housed in separate "colored barracks" several blocks away.

When the Ponce de Leon was completed in May 1887, skeptics doubted that the $2,500,000 complex would ever attract enough people to make it profitable. The hotel opened in January for the winter season of 1888 with hundreds of America's wealthiest and most celebrated citizens in attendance. Flagler had succeeded. For half a decade, the Ponce de Leon was the most exclusive winter resort in the nation.

The fashionable crowd is always a fickle one. After only ten years, the Ponce de Leon and its sister hotel began to undergo a steady decline in their fortunes. The depression that crippled the nation's finances in 1893 sharply reduced vacation travel. The sophisticated resorters who did come found life in old Saint Augustine rather dull. Part of the problem was Flagler's own expansion of his railroad and hotel empire down Florida's east coast and the steady competition on its west coast from other developers. Saint Augustine soon became merely a brief stop en route to the sunnier clime of Palm Beach, the winter Newport.

The hotels of Saint Augustine did experience renewed prosperity during the first decade of the twentieth century, the period of restricted European travel during World War I, and the Florida land boom of the 1920s. But long before the Crash of 1929, the Saint Augustine hotels were again operating at a deficit as tourists drove on through to Miami and Fort Lauderdale. For a time, the Casino baths housed a speakeasy, with live-in ladies of ill fame offering patrons diverse amusements. During the dark days of the Depression, the Ponce de Leon averaged a mere forty guests a day, while the Alcazar closed altogether. The Coast Guard leased the Ponce de Leon as a training facility to save it from financial ruin during World War II.

The end of the war brought a brief resurgence of prosperity, but the Ponce de Leon began once again to lose patronage. Few tourists cared to spend time in northern Florida, and fewer still chose to stray beyond the new hotels that lined Route 1. In 1948, Chicagoan O. C. Lightner, the editor of Hobbies magazine, reopened the Alcazar as a museum. The building now also houses the offices of the City of Saint Augustine. After operating for eighty years as a hotel, the Ponce de Leon closed its doors in 1967. The gleaming walls and grand spaces that once sheltered the cream of American society now provide a home for the students of Flagler College.

Left, above: The main dining room of the Ponce de Leon Hotel.
Left, below: Tennis players on the Alcazar courts
Above: The plan of the Ponce de Leon and the Alcazar

TAMPA BAY HOTEL
Tampa, Florida

All successful men have their rivals, and Henry Flagler was no exception. While Flagler was developing the east coast of Florida into an American tropical paradise, Henry Bradley Plant was extending his railroad and steamship empire down Florida's west coast. When the rails of the Plant system reached Tampa in 1880, it was a tiny community of 800 people. Twelve years later the population had risen to 10,000, and by the mid-1890s it was a growing town supported by, among other things, 130 cigar factories—certainly a thriving industry. With South Florida Railroad connections to the North and with Plant-system steamship connections to Cuba, Tampa also became a transportation hub and a thriving city.

Like Flagler, Plant realized the advantages of developing accommodations to serve his transportation system, and purchased land on Tampa Bay with the intention of building a hotel. To increase accessibility to the site, he persuaded the city to construct a bridge across the Hillsborough River. Though Plant's decision to build away from the center of town had been unpopular with the town's merchants, his architect, J. A. Wood of New York, felt the waterside site to be a more suitable setting for the new "Alhambra" he intended to create. When the Tampa Bay Hotel opened on January 31, 1891, Flagler reportedly sent a jesting telegram inquiring, "Where is Tampa?" Plant's reply: "Just follow the crowds!"

Plant had also followed Flagler's lead in adopting a Moorish-Mediterranean architectural style as a way of recalling Florida's romantic Spanish past. Thirteen silver-roofed minarets and other exotic touches, including keyhole windows and wooden tracery on the extensive verandas, gave his hotel an edge over Flagler's for sheer audacity and exuberance. The huge structure was built of buff-colored brick with steel supports consisting largely of rails, which were being replaced on Plant's railroad lines at the time and were readily available.

The interior of the hotel was equally grand and exotic, but there the specifically Moorish architectural theme gave way to a richer eclecticism. The two-story lobby boasted a perimeter gallery supported by granite columns. The main dining room was a rotunda articulated by keyhole arches and decorated with murals depicting the history of Spanish Florida. Paintings and sculpture from Plant's own collection adorned the galleries and sitting rooms. Plant used European antiques as tangible proof of his good taste and great wealth; some pieces were said to have belonged to Ferdinand and Isabella, to Mary Queen of Scots, to Louis Philippe, and to Marie Antoinette. Even the table service in the dining room was a medley of patterns reproduced from French, English, and Austrian originals. Mr. and Mrs. Plant had acquired much of the furniture and artwork for the hotel on a European buying spree in 1889. They were especially proud of their bargain purchase of several acres of carpet bearing the lion-rampant motif used exclusively by English royalty. A pamphlet published by the Plant system summarized the uniqueness of the Tampa Bay Hotel by comparing it with its contemporaries: "The others boast of their especially made appointments, while these were made before the land was discovered." The time-honored furnishings in combination with the exotic architectural shell certainly created an atmosphere of opulence and grandeur in keeping with the tastes and passions of the late nineteenth century.

The hotel served as a resting spot and playground for vacationers and for performers and dignitaries traveling to and from Cuba. Anna Pavlova, William Jennings Bryan, Babe Ruth, Clara Barton, and Stephen Crane were among its famous guests. Mrs. Theodore Roosevelt stayed there during the Spanish-American War while Teddy trained with his troops on the grounds in preparation for the American invasion of Cuba.

After Plant's death in 1899, the Tampa Bay Hotel was sold to the City of Tampa. For the next twenty years it remained the social center of Tampa even though it faltered financially under various lessees. In 1920, W. F. Adams acquired the lease, rehabilitated the hotel, and enjoyed the fruits of Florida's greatest boom period. But the Depression brought prosperity to an end, and the gigantic structure became a gigantic liability. Fortunately, the Tampa Bay Hotel was saved from destruction when the University of Tampa took over the building in 1933. Its major rooms have since been restored and still suggest to the contemporary visitor their original character and magnificence.

The silver-domed Tampa Bay Hotel now houses the University of Tampa.

Dinner —
✳ ✳

Canapé, à la Gage

BLUE POINTS

Cream of Artichaut, à la Reine
Clear Green Turtle aux Quenelles   Essence of Chicken in Cup, Brunoise

Salted Almonds   Olives   Celery   Caviar   Brandy Peaches

Filet of Shad Planked, à l'Amiral
Broiled Smelts au Beurre, Montpellier
Potatoes, Julienne   Sliced Cucumbers

Timbal of Chicken, Lagardère

Diamond-Back Terrapin, à la Newburg
Sweetbreads Sur Croûte, à la Delmonico
Breast of Chicken Fried, Sauce Hongroise
Filet of Beef Larded, Sauce Perigeux
Spaghetti, à la Camerani

Cold Asparagus, Vinaigrette ——— Paté de Foie Gras, Strasbourgeoise
Vermont Turkey Stuffed, with Chestnuts
Ribs of Prime Beef   Spring Lamb, Mint sauce
New Green Peas   New String Beans   Mashed Potatoes
Boiled New Potatoes   New Beets   Sweet Potatoes, Brown
Boiled Rice   Cauliflower, Cream sauce   Stewed Celery

PUNCH, Á LA POINCIANA

Red Head Duck, Guava Jelly
Fried Hominy

Chicken Salad   Celery   Lettuce and Tomato   Lobster Salad

Croûte aux Bananas, à la Crêole

Plum Pudding, Hard and Brandy sauce
Pudding, à la Richelieu, Champagne sauce
Apple Pie   Pumpkin Pie   Mince Pie
Strawberry Eclairs   Petits Bouchées en Surprise   Gateaux, Assortie
Baton de Paris   Fancy Iced Cake
Vanilla Macaroons   Chocolate Africaines
Charlotte Russe   Petit Fours   Jelly au Kirsch

VANILLA ICE CREAM   BISCUIT GLACÉE

Bananas   Apples   Figs   Dates   Oranges
Assorted Nuts   Malaga Grapes   Layer Raisins

CHEESE—Edam   Cream   Pineapple
Roquefort   American

Toasted Water Crackers
COFFEE

THURSDAY, FEBRUARY 22, 1900   DINNER, 6.30 TO 8.00

Supper will be Served in the Palm Room Tonight from Eleven to One o'clock

THE ROYAL POINCIANA

Palm Beach, Florida

Palm Beach was still a sparsely settled peninsula when Henry Flagler first visited it in the early 1890s. Its wonderful climate and lush tropical growth seemed to suggest a paradise on earth, ripe for profitable development. So it was that Flagler bought a sizable tract of land there in 1893 and announced his intention to build another addition to his growing chain of resort hotels. Obviously this meant the extension of Flagler's railroad system farther south, and news of that sent real estate prices soaring. The few landowners who had settled on Palm Beach suddenly found themselves sitting on the gold mine that was to become Florida's Gold Coast.

Construction of the hotel began on May 1, 1893, and a makeshift shantytown called Styx immediately sprang up around the construction site to house the workers. Because the railroad extension and the hotel were under construction at the same time, materials for the building had to be brought in by steamer. The new hotel was to be called the Royal Poinciana after a beautiful flowering plant that grows wild there. Ironically, visitors to the hotel never saw these summer bloomers in their full glory.

A resort of the size Flagler intended would obviously need support facilities and housing for its gigantic staff. While the hotel was being built, the workers' community of West Palm Beach was established on the inland shore of Lake Worth, far enough from the grounds of the hotel to preserve its exclusive atmosphere.

The Royal Poinciana opened on February 11, 1894, and immediately became a mecca for the nation's wealthy. Rail connections were completed in April of the same year, and with the construction of a bridge across Lake Worth, guests could step from the comforts of a private palace car to the hotel's entrance. As many as 100 private railroad cars would arrive each season. After discharging their owners, they would be rolled to the rear of the building as housing for the servants, thereby saving hotel rooms.

The Royal Poinciana was widely praised both for the beauties of its vast tropical gardens and beaches and for the appearance of the building itself. Its style was the typical Georgian Revival of the period, with the requisite Ionic columns and classical moldings. The clapboard exterior was painted "Flagler yellow" and the veran-

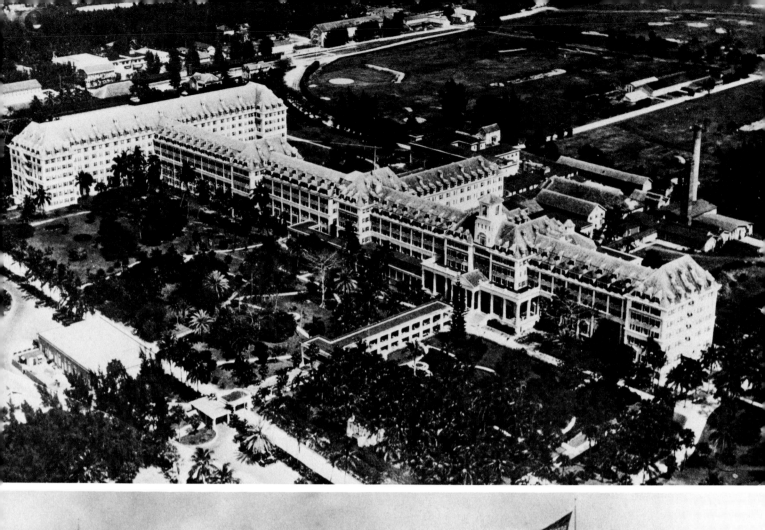

Left: The immense Royal Poinciana (above), with guests
posed before one of the side railings, where their private
cars are parked (below)
Above: Afromobiles awaiting passengers

das, window frames balconies, and trim were white. Most of
its architectural interest centered upon its size: it was the largest
wooden building ever erected. The E-shaped six-story structure
had 3 miles of corridors, requiring its less energetic visitors to
make use of single-seated wicker carts—called "Afromobiles"—
pedaled about the corridors and grounds by black hotel employees.
The corridors themselves were as wide as streets and were lined
with shops that could easily have graced New York's Fifth Avenue.
The interior color scheme was green and white with a profusion
of velvet-upholstered furniture and potted palms. Henry James, an
enthusiastic observer of the Royal Poinciana, found its primary
interest to be his fellow guests:

**The boarders, verily, were the great indicated show as I had gathered in
advance, at Palm Beach; it had been promised one, on all sides, that there,
as nowhere else in America, one would find Vanity Fair in full blast—and
Vanity Fair not scattered, not discriminated and parcelled out, as among the
comparative privacies and ancestries of Newport, but compressed under one
vast cover, enclosed in a single huge vitrine, which there would be nothing
to prevent one's flattening one's nose against for days of delight.**

It must indeed have been a marvelous spectacle, with everyone
dressed to the nines. A tremendous wardrobe was a prerequisite
for a stay at the Royal Poinciana: appropriate apparel was essential for breakfast, morning strolls, bathing, boating, luncheon,
bicycling, golf, tea, afternoon strolls, supper, evening promenades,
and dancing. One dared not repeat an outfit too often. Because the
average stay lasted a number of weeks, trunkloads of clothing
accompanied each guest.

The hotel's wealthy patronage—a suite could cost $100 a day in
the 1890s—provided the ideal atmosphere for social climbers as
well. Indeed, a great number of affluent new rich with an eye on
social acceptance did hope to make the step up at Palm Beach.
But there as at old Saratoga, proximity to the elite was no guar-
antee of social success. The point is well illustrated by a story
from Ring Lardner's Gullible's Travels. An upward-mobile couple
have come to Palm Beach to meet the elite, but all they have
received for their efforts and a great deal of money is a speaking
acquaintance with the maid. Finally the Missus is approached by
the Mrs. Potter from Chicago in the hallway outside their room:

**"Are you on this floor?" she asks. The Missus shook like a leaf. "Yes," says
she, so low you couldn't hardly hear her. "Please see that there are some
towels put in 559," says the Mrs. Potter from Chicago.**

The Royal Poinciana operated until 1931, although it suffered
from ill repair and a reduced clientele in the years after the
collapse of the Florida real estate boom in the 1920s. Severe
damage was inflicted by a hurricane in 1934, and the hotel had to
be torn down.

BELLEVIEW-BILTMORE HOTEL

Belleair, Florida

The Belleview-Biltmore Hotel, known affectionately as the "White Queen of the Gulf," formally opened January 15, 1897, for the winter season, with fifteen private railroad cars filling to capacity the special rail siding. In all the years since, the hotel has claimed to be one of the largest occupied wooden structures in the world. The statistics are awesome: 450 rooms, 2 miles of hallways, 3,000 meals served daily at peak season. The accommodations have been excellent from the beginning. An 1898 brochure noted that

every bedroom has three incandescent lights, a mantel of polished cedar with handsome tiling surrounding the fireplace, polished floors, and oak or cherry furniture. There are several suites of rooms with bath connected.

The hotel was built by Henry Plant as part of the chain of resorts on the west coast of Florida that was served by his railroad. One could stop at Boca Grande, Punta Gorda, Fort Myers, or Tampa Bay and be in the care of Plant's hotels. Plant spared no expense on the Belleview. It was made deliberately lavish to drum up business on the railroad line and to compete with the resorts being created by Flagler on the east coast.

The most interesting aspect of the Belleview today, apart from its fin de siècle wooden architecture, is that its turn-of-the-century atmosphere is also intact, with many of the guests still checking in for the entire season. Typical features of bygone resorts, such as elaborate daily menus, elegant table service, and even a stuffily quiet round of activities, are still very much present. A stay at the Belleview is curiously like stepping back into the past.

HOTEL DEL MONTE
Monterey, California

By the mid-1870s, promoters of the Monterey Peninsula were well aware that Eastern-style tourist hotels would attract potential investors to the area. The Western railroads were also alert to the opportunity to enhance the value of their holdings while generating business on their lines. Through its subsidiary, the Pacific Improvement Company, Charles Crocker's Southern Pacific Railroad decided to build an elegant hotel not far from the old town of Monterey. The railroad had already acquired some 7,000 acres of land surrounding the town, and its operators lost no time in capitalizing on their investment. In September 1880, the Hotel Del Monte opened for business. It catered to San Francisco's elite, who assured the venture's success when they claimed the resort as their own. Not everyone was pleased. Robert Louis Stevenson, then staying in old Monterey, wrote:

A huge hotel has sprung up in the desert by the railway. Three sets of diners sit down successively to table. Invaluable toilettes figure along the beach and between the live oaks; and Monterey is advertised in the newspapers and posted in the waiting rooms at railway stations as a resort for wealth and fashion. Alas for the little town! It is not strong enough to resist the influence of the flaunting caravanserai, and the poor, quaint, penniless native gentlemen of Monterey must perish, like a lower race, before the millionaire vulgarians of the Big Bonanza.

True to the pattern in other parts of the West, the hotel builders took little note of the area's "backward" Spanish past. The architectural style, which soothingly catered to Eastern expectations, was an amalgam of the "Swiss" Stick Style and Queen Anne, with towers and turrets, lacy stickwork verandas, and half-timbering. Its lobby was likened to that of the Grand Union at Saratoga. The parade of officers from nearby military installations recalled the social scene at Newport. Even the gardens were modeled on English precedents. The first Eastern tourists took the hotel's apparent informality as fact and appeared in informal traveling clothes. They were shocked to find themselves snubbed by the San Franciscans, whose provincial position and new money led them to be even more fiercely snobbish and style-conscious than their counterparts in the East.

The hotel's stickwork verandas and trim, its irregular massing, and its polychrome roof tiles are components of the Queen Anne Style.

Turn-of-the-century cyclists at rest before the wooden verandas of the Hotel Del Monte

Only seven years after its completion, the Del Monte was destroyed by fire. San Francisco architect A. Page Brown, who had been brought to California by the Crocker interests, designed a bigger hotel for the same spot. It too was "Swiss." The front façade was composed of three tall pavilions, linked by horizontal dormered wings to create an irregular profile. Verandas stretched across the entire building. Because fire was a major concern, the kitchen was placed at the garden end of the long dining room to isolate it from the main structure. The guest rooms were in wings also placed at a distance from the main building and connected to it only by long curving colonnades that could be dynamited to provide fire breaks.

The hotel's expanded and lavishly landscaped park included sweeping lawns, splashes of floral color, and gnarled cypress trees and oaks—"26 acres of paradise." A golf course, a polo field, a race track, and tennis courts provided facilities for aristocratic sports. For those who found bathing in Monterey Bay or the Pacific Ocean too chilly, there was an immense glass-enclosed bathing pavilion with heated fresh-water and salt-water pools. A romantic

Indoor bathing pavilion at the Del Monte

seventeen-mile drive wound through the Del Monte forest to Pebble Beach, Cypress Point, and the marine gardens at the nearby Methodist retreat of Pacific Grove.

For all its attractions, the popularity of the Del Monte waned after the turn of the century. Its management insisted on maintaining out-of-date social decorum, such as overly formal dress codes, which made the hotel seem downright stuffy to younger guests. By 1915, the hotel had deteriorated noticeably and was no longer realizing a satisfactory profit for its owners. Therefore, the Crockers asked their business representative, young Samuel F. B. Morse, grandson of the inventor, to liquidate the Pacific Improvement Company's holdings at Del Monte. Morse, with the help of San Francisco banker Herbert Fleishhacker, organized the Del Monte Properties Corporation, which purchased the hotel and the Crocker family's extensive landholdings. Within a year, under new management, the hotel revived. A new lodge was built at Pebble Beach. The seventeen-mile drive was improved and completed, and hundreds of miles of bridle trails were developed in the Del Monte forest above Carmel. Morse had hit upon the notion of using Del Monte Properties as a grand real estate scheme that operated much like a private country club. The purchase of a lot entitled the new owner to full use of the extensive facilities of the hotel. This promotional scheme was so successful that in 1924, when the main wing of the hotel was again destroyed by fire, there were enough funds to renovate the entire complex and to add a new $2,000,000 main building. The latter was in the Mediterranean Style, as an expression of the new romantic interest in Monterey's Spanish colonial heritage. Even the old "Swiss" wings of the original hotel were given a coat of white paint and red roofs to bring them visually up-to-date. Architects Louis Hobart and Clarence Tantau designed the new reinforced-concrete building with an exceptionally tall first floor and a long, extended plan to give it grandeur.

Once again the Del Monte prospered, but its flush days were numbered. The Depression dealt it a severe blow. Although Del Monte Properties managed to keep afloat by selling land and catering to club members and convention groups, the hotel still lost money. With the outbreak of World War II, the Del Monte was leased to the United States Navy as a training center. The government then bought the hotel together with 600 acres of land. Today the Del Monte houses the Navy Postgraduate School at Monterey.

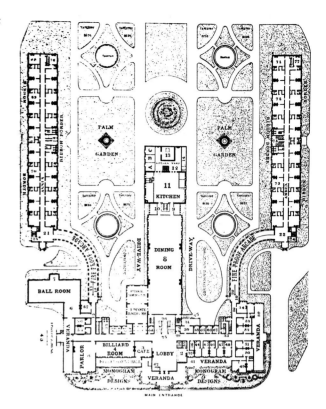

Above: Ground-floor plan of the Del Monte showing curved fire-break arcades
Right, above: Tennis players between sets
Right, below: In its vast size the dining room of the Del Monte was typical of the period. The carved wooden ceiling brackets recall the trim on the hotel's exterior.

HOTEL DEL CORONADO - CORONADO.

HOTEL DEL CORONADO

Coronado, California

The Hotel Del Coronado is the last of the many grand resorts that once dotted the California coast. Still standing intact and indeed still operating successfully as a hotel after nearly a century, the building was named a State Historical Landmark in 1970, was listed in the National Register of Historic Places in 1971, and became a National Historic Landmark in 1977. The <u>fin de siècle</u> splendor of the building now seems more important than ever.

The hotel is sited prominently at the north end of a long narrow spit of land called the Silver Strand, which separates and protects San Diego harbor from the Pacific Ocean. From the sea, it resembles a sprawling white castle or a large white rock. At the time it was built, it must have suggested the sublime marriage of architecture and landscape which Americans found so pleasing in Europe and so lacking at home. Although recent condominium development has encroached upon the hotel, for most of its long life its guests were treated to incomparable views of the harbor and ocean and of mesas and high mountains forty miles away. An early visitor noted that guests carried away

the memory of sunsets emblazoned in gold and crimson upon cloud, sea, and mountains; of violet promontories, sails, and lighthouses etched against the orange of a western sky . . . of distant islands shimmering in sun-lit haze, or sunrises . . . chasing the vapory, fleece-like shadows from the wet iridescent beach, and silhouetting the fisherman's sails in the opalescent tints of a glossy sea.

The spectacular site and the benign climate, together with the flamboyant and exotic wooden building, created an ambience which has connoted luxury through nearly a century of rapidly changing cultural values.

At the turn of the century, industrial barons arrived at the "Del" in private railroad cars. In 1920, the Prince of Wales, that devoted patron of resort hotels, added his cachet by attending a banquet in his honor at which he allegedly met his future wife, Wallis Warfield Simpson. During the 1930s and 1940s, the hotel was one of the favored playgrounds of the Hollywood movie colony and the natural place to reside when playing the gaming tables at the Agua Caliente Casino across the border.

The entrance of the flamboyantly Victorian hotel, with the eleven-sided ballroom at the left and the Pacific Ocean just beyond

Above: The Del Coronado served as a catalyst for the development of Coronado Beach. As shown in this map, the hotel was built and trees were planted before many lots were sold. Below: Thatched cottages and tents provided inexpensive accommodations in the "tent city" adjacent to the hotel.

The completion of the southern transcontinental railroad link to Southern California and to San Diego in 1885 gave Easterners their first taste of a Mediterranean climate and initiated a land boom of unprecedented proportions in the region. Across the harbor from San Diego, then a small city of less than 10,000 people, lay the untouched Coronado Peninsula, a barren windswept parcel of 4,100 acres inhabited mostly by jack rabbits, coyotes, and wildcats. The entire parcel was purchased in December 1885 by Elisha S. Babcock, a retired railroad executive from Evansville, Indiana, and H. L. Story of the Story and Clark Piano Company of Chicago. The Coronado Beach Company was quickly established, the land subdivided, and lots offered for sale. Among the many improvements that the developers promised was the construction of a hotel that would be "the talk of the Western world." As if an extraordinary hotel itself was not a sufficient attraction to boost land sales, gimmicks such as balloon ascensions and free ferryboat and streetcar travel to San Diego were also offered.

Construction of the hotel began in March 1887. There was no time to prepare plans, and the architects, James and Merritt Reid, who had never designed such a large hotel before, stayed one step ahead of the workers by preparing sketches each night for the next day's construction. The vast amount of wood required was supplied by the Dolbeer and Cardon Lumber Company of San Francisco. It was barged down from the north, and planed and finished right on the site in a specially constructed planing mill. There were an ironworks and a metal shop on the site, and a brick kiln that produced all the brick used in the construction. To supplement the local and mostly unskilled laborers, a large number of Chinese workers were supplied by the Chinese Seven Companies, an influential group of San Francisco families. To ease the problems of building such an extensive and complicated structure with largely unskilled labor, the architects began with the simplest wings, allowing the crews to gain experience before they tackled the ingenious and difficult structures that enclose the ballroom and dining room. Construction of the building cost $600,000, with another $400,000 expended on furnishings. Eighty freight cars were required to bring the original, specially made furniture to the hotel, while another train brought 324 people from the East to form the hotel staff. The hotel was completed and open for business only eleven months later, on February 19, 1888. Babcock drummed up patronage by announcing that

there is not any malaria, hay-fever, sleeplessness, loss of appetite, or languor in the air; nor any thunder, lightning, mad dogs, cyclones, heated-terms, or cold-snaps—and all these advantages may be enjoyed for $3.00 per day and upward.

Lobby of the Del Coronado in the 1930s. The crown logo here takes the form of a chandelier.

Despite the absence of formal plans, the Del Coronado is not a casual, rambling structure, nor is it based on an overly simple, repetitive system of rooms. The building has a clearly organized plan enlivened by irregular, picturesque form. The guest rooms are grouped on three sides of the courtyard, with all public rooms on the southern side. The clarity of the scheme results in part from owner-developer Babcock's sensitive understanding of how to use the site. His charge to the architects was that the hotel

be built around a court … a garden of tropical trees, shrubs, and flowers. From the south end, the foyer should open to Glorietta Bay with verandas for rest and promenade. On the ocean corner, there should be a pavilion tower, and northward along the ocean, a colonnade, terraced in grass to the beach. The dining wing should project at an angle from the southeast corner of the court, and be almost detached to give full value to the view of the ocean, bay, and city.

Although variously called a High Victorian or Queen Anne building, the hotel was distinguished from most of its contemporaries by its color scheme: the white walls and red shingle roof were obvious attempts to evoke the Spanish colonial heritage of the region. Thus, the hotel combined Eastern and local building traditions to create an architectural image that appealed to Eastern visitors because it was both familiar and exotic.

The hotel is dominated by three extraordinary spaces: the one-acre enclosed courtyard, once inhabited by exotic and rather noisy birds and monkeys and a profusion of tropical plants; the immense dining room, capable of seating 1,000; and the circular ballroom, big enough to accommodate 1,200 dancers. The courtyard is enclosed on four sides, forming a setting for a tropical landscape completely removed, visually, from the windswept peninsula upon which the building is situated. Resort hotels of this period usually had a manicured park or garden adjacent to the structure, and courtyards, where they existed, opened on the sea or some other natural wonder. At the Del Coronado the entire surrounding landscape, though awesome, was also barren and therefore not the primary attraction. Yet the climate suggested paradise, and so the courtyard enclosed an arcadian vision, a fantasy landscape to complement the climate.

The dining room, 156 feet long, 62 feet wide, and 33 feet high, has no columns to mar the open sweep of space. Its elegantly vaulted ceiling is constructed of sugar pine, using only wooden pegs and no nails. Once a year, the staff musters rags, ladders, and gallons of furniture polish to keep the wood in good condition. The conical ballroom with its panoramic view of the ocean was no doubt the most visually arresting space of the early Del Coronado. Unfortunately, lowering the ceiling to accommodate air conditioning has robbed the room of much of its impact, although it is the only regrettable compromise required by present standards of comfort.

Originally there were 73 baths and 399 rooms, each with a fireplace and wall safe and each in some way unique. The fireplaces were supplanted by a steam-heating system in 1896, and over the years every room has acquired a private bath. It is important to note that, unlike most of its contemporaries, the Del Coronado was a complete entity from the beginning and still retains the original 399 rooms in a plan that worked so well that additions were not required until recently. These new accommodations have been placed in separate buildings at a respectful distance from the main structure.

A "Tent City," built to the south of the hotel, provided auxiliary lodgings as well as a race track, boating facilities, and an ostrich farm. The tents and thatched huts, renting for a mere $2.75 per week unfurnished or $6.00 per week furnished, gave a less affluent clientele their place in the sun. Special entertainment and exciting but respectable diversions such as rodeos, concerts, and parades also occurred there, until the Tent City was demolished in the early 1940s.

For those guests who arrived in their private railroad cars, there was a siding in front of the hotel. Local newspaper accounts described with awe the arrival of the "floury Pillsburys, the yeasty Fleischmanns, and the billiard-rich Bensingers." A hotel bus was dispatched to collect guests who came by ferryboat from San Diego. The Del Coronado, whose balconies and galleries afforded, in Henry James's phrase, "space sufficient to air all the guests simultaneously," also claimed to be the first hotel and the largest building outside of New York City to have electric lighting, an assertion hotly contested by Henry Flagler's Ponce de Leon Hotel in Saint Augustine, Florida.

The Hotel Del Coronado is a survivor from another age, and its survival has been dependent not only upon careful management but also upon the relative isolation of the town of Coronado. In 1969, a bridge was built connecting the town with San Diego, thus irrevocably altering Coronado's sleepy atmosphere. Looking west from the top of that bridge into the haze of the setting sun, the hotel looms on the horizon like a pile of dark, craggy rocks, with the low domestic town to the north and multistoried apartment slabs to the south. Had the bridge been built earlier, the hotel doubtless would have succumbed to the development pressures of an age that cared little for old buildings. While many revere the Del Coronado for its nostalgic lore and glamorous past associations, it is far more appropriate to value and enjoy the place for what it is: a remarkably moving and successful and delightful piece of architecture.

Above: Garden courtyard at the Del Coronado
Right: Ground-floor plan
Far right: Second-floor plan

Qourt · Hotel Del Coronado.

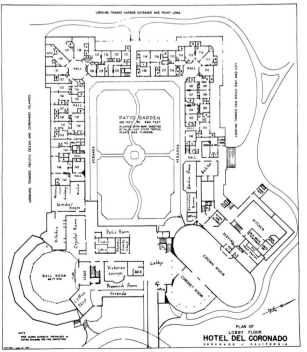

PLAN OF
LOBBY FLOOR
HOTEL DEL CORONADO
CORONADO — CALIFORNIA

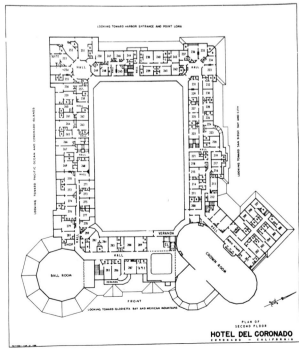

PLAN OF
SECOND FLOOR
HOTEL DEL CORONADO
CORONADO — CALIFORNIA

GALVESTON BEACH HOTEL

Galveston, Texas

The Galveston Beach Hotel was fated to have a short life. It opened with a grand celebration on July 3, 1883, and burned to the ground on the morning of July 23, 1898. During its fifteen-year life it offered first-class hotel accommodations right on the beach to wealthy Texans on vacation.

Clearly the largest building in town, the hotel contained 200 rooms on three floors. Its ground plan resembled a letter E with the legs turned to the ocean to take advantage of the slightest cool breeze blowing in off the Gulf of Mexico. Verandas 18 feet in depth extended along the full 245 feet of the E and on both sides for 112 feet. Perhaps the most distinctive feature of the hotel was its vivid polychrome surfaces. The roof was painted in giant red and white stripes. The structure itself was painted mauve, with the eaves a golden green. The dome was painted in several bright colors. The hotel was a dazzling sight along the oceanfront, and never more so than as it burned.

The vast interior of the Saltair was supported by thin metal trusses of a type most often associated with train sheds.

SALTAIR
Great Salt Lake, Utah

Although Saltair was not a hotel, it was the focus of resort activity around Salt Lake City. Like Coney Island's Luna Park, it seemed to capture the essence of carefree seaside fantasy.

Saltair was built in 1894 by the Salt Lake and Los Angeles Railroad, which was in turn owned by the Mormon Church. The complex stood on piles far out in Great Salt Lake and was reached via a railroad causeway 4,000 feet long. The water in that part of the lake was four-and-a-half feet deep—perfect for bathing from the promenades at the building's lowest level. The first floor was one large room devoted to picnicking and restaurants; a vast dance hall was sheltered under the domed roof above. The Oriental character of the building was intended to recall the magic and mystery of the Arabian Nights.

Saltair was very popular, but it had its problems as well. In 1901, its concessionaires stirred up a storm of protest by selling beer in open defiance of the Sunday closing laws. The embarrassed church fathers put things right by selling the resort to a group of teetotaling Mormon managers. The resort held its own until it was destroyed by fire in 1925.

C.R.SAVAGE.PHOTO.

A promenade flanked the many-domed Saltair pavilion.

LAKEFRONT, SALTAIR BEACH, GT. SALT L

MONTEZUMA HOTEL
Las Vegas Hot Springs, New Mexico

The Las Vegas Hot Springs were renowned for their curative powers long before the United States Army erected a small adobe hospital there in 1846. When the military moved on in 1862, the building became a hotel. The Santa Fe Railway reached Las Vegas in 1879, and the Hot Springs Hotel was constructed in the same year. Built of local sandstone, it had extensive verandas and a central tower with a mansard roof. Bathhouses were also constructed so that visitors could partake of the mud baths and mineral waters in reasonable comfort. A cottage colony soon developed. The success of the Hot Springs as a resort convinced the Santa Fe Railway to build a spur line from the town of Las Vegas, about six miles to the south. The railroad also formed the Las Vegas Hot Springs Company, bought the existing hotel, and made plans to build a new one.

The Montezuma Hotel opened its doors to health-seekers on April 17, 1882, an oasis of comfort and familiar Eastern gentility amid the rugged Sangre de Cristo mountains. Broad sweeping lawns, shade trees and flower gardens surrounded a Queen Anne Style building that contained all the conveniences and luxuries that resorters had come to expect. But the Montezuma also held a few surprises for the weary traveler. The cuisine was under the direction of Santa Fe concessionaire Fred Harvey, the "Lucullus of the West," whose excellent food and courteous service were a match for most Eastern restaurants. The cool dry air and the delights of board and bath made the resort a place where the infirm came to get well and the healthy came to enjoy themselves.

An interesting glimpse into the life of the hotel is offered by George G. Street, who visited the Montezuma in 1883. After an excellent dinner and an evening of dancing and flirtation that lasted until well after midnight, when the Montezuma Ideals chorus sang "Good Night, Ladies," the intrepid tourist was up with the sun to enjoy a Russian bath before breakfast. After tickling the feet of hapless friends in steam cabinets, Street allowed himself to be placed in the "stocks."

A thousand jolts of hot water suddenly strike you like needles from all directions and the boiling process begins. You gradually feel yourself melting away and wonder how much of you will be left to take home to your family.

But before he had totally dissolved, Street was set free, only to be doused with hot and cold water.

You are laid on a marble slab, drenched with soapsuds, scrubbed with a brush until you think that the attendant has mistaken you for a pine floor....
Your joints are pulled, twisted and bent, dislocated and re-set, and after being drowned once or twice more you are rubbed down with dry towels.

Street enjoyed the experience nonetheless.

Going again into the open air, you feel like a bird, fly across the bridge, prance around the balcony, and then enjoy the best and biggest breakfast you ever had, seasoned with a smile from the brightest pair of eyes in the room, the belle of the evening before having graciously been pleased to offer you a smile.

In 1884 the Montezuma was destroyed by fire. But with the popularity of the Hot Springs a proven fact, the Santa Fe Railway commissioned Burnham and Root of Chicago to design a second hotel on the site. Daniel Hudson Burnham contributed some conceptual sketches to the project, but the hotel was actually designed by John Wellborn Root. Burnham had visited the Hot Springs, and in his journal of 1883 he spoke of the exhilarating effects of the steam baths. Although Root never did visit the site, he was able to design a building in which Eastern efficiency and sophistication were provided within an architectural setting in sympathy with the landscape. As his biographer, Harriet Moore, expressed it:

Here the low building seems to grow out of the very rocks from which its wide projecting roof slants upward. The generous welcome it offers, the sense of shelter from invading storms, the absolute fitness of every line and feature of it, make this far-away inn one of the most exquisite idylls its author ever dreamed.

Although every room contained an alarm system and every precaution was taken against fire, the upper portions of the Montezuma burned on August 9, 1885. The local fire brigade managed to save only the wine cellar—for themselves. Once again the hotel was rebuilt, reopening in 1886 as the Phoenix. Out of habit and affection, however, it continued to be known as the Montezuma.

Unfortunately neither the healing power of the springs, the appeal of the building itself, nor even its location just off the main rail line to Southern California helped to bolster sagging revenues as competition from other Western resorts began to draw the patrons away. The Montezuma was forced to close in 1893. Subsequent attempts at revitalization failed. For a time the building was occupied by a Mexican seminary, but now it stands empty, a prey to vandals and to natural decay.

Guests relaxing beneath the spray of the hot springs fountain at the Montezuma

018142. THE RENDEVOUS, HOTEL EL TOVAR,

EL TOVAR

Grand Canyon National Park, Arizona

El Tovar was named for Don Pedro de Tovar, a lieutenant of the Spanish explorer Francisco de Coronado. When Tovar learned of the Grand Canyon from the Hopi Indians, he told Coronado, who immediately sent out members of his party to verify the tale. For the next three centuries, however, the canyon was ignored by everyone except local Indians. Then in 1869, Major John Wesley Powell rediscovered the Grand Canyon on a boat trip down the rapids and waterfalls of the Colorado River. In 1884, the Santa Fe Railway made the Grand Canyon accessible to visitors from both coasts.

El Tovar was built by the railroad in 1901, on a spectacular site at the rim of the canyon a mile above the Colorado River. The building was designed to harmonize with its rugged setting. Its architect, Charles F. Whittlesey of Chicago, described it as resembling a "Norwegian villa," with base and chimneys of native limestone and upper walls faced with logs and shingles. The soft greys and greens of roof and walls allowed the building to blend with the surrounding trees. The interior was appropriately rustic as well. The original furnishings were in the Arts and Crafts mode. Moose heads and Indian crafts decorated the walls. Typical guest rooms had rough sand-finished walls and ceilings and dark simple woodwork. Despite the hotel's apparent rusticity, its management went to great lengths to assure the public that it was in fact fully modern, to the point of including photographs and facts concerning the water system and basement laundry plant in their advertising brochures. But for those patrons who preferred a more "civilized" environment, certain suites were given an Eastern flavor through the use of mahogany furniture, floral wallpaper, and carpeting.

El Tovar was carefully planned to make the most of its site. Each room has at least a partial view of the canyon. The service rooms are placed away from the rim. The dining room and its porches project forward from the main building, providing them with a particularly spectacular 180-degree view of the canyon. The guest wings radiate out from a central octagonal lobby just behind the dining room. Both wings end in public rooms that have a panoramic view. As one delighted tourist noted, the guest hardly needed to go outside to enjoy nature's wonders. For the more adventurous, excursions down into the canyon by burro and horse left from the front door on a regular schedule.

Trophy heads, Indian blankets, and hand-crafted furniture enhance the rustic architecture in the Rendezvous Lounge at El Tovar.

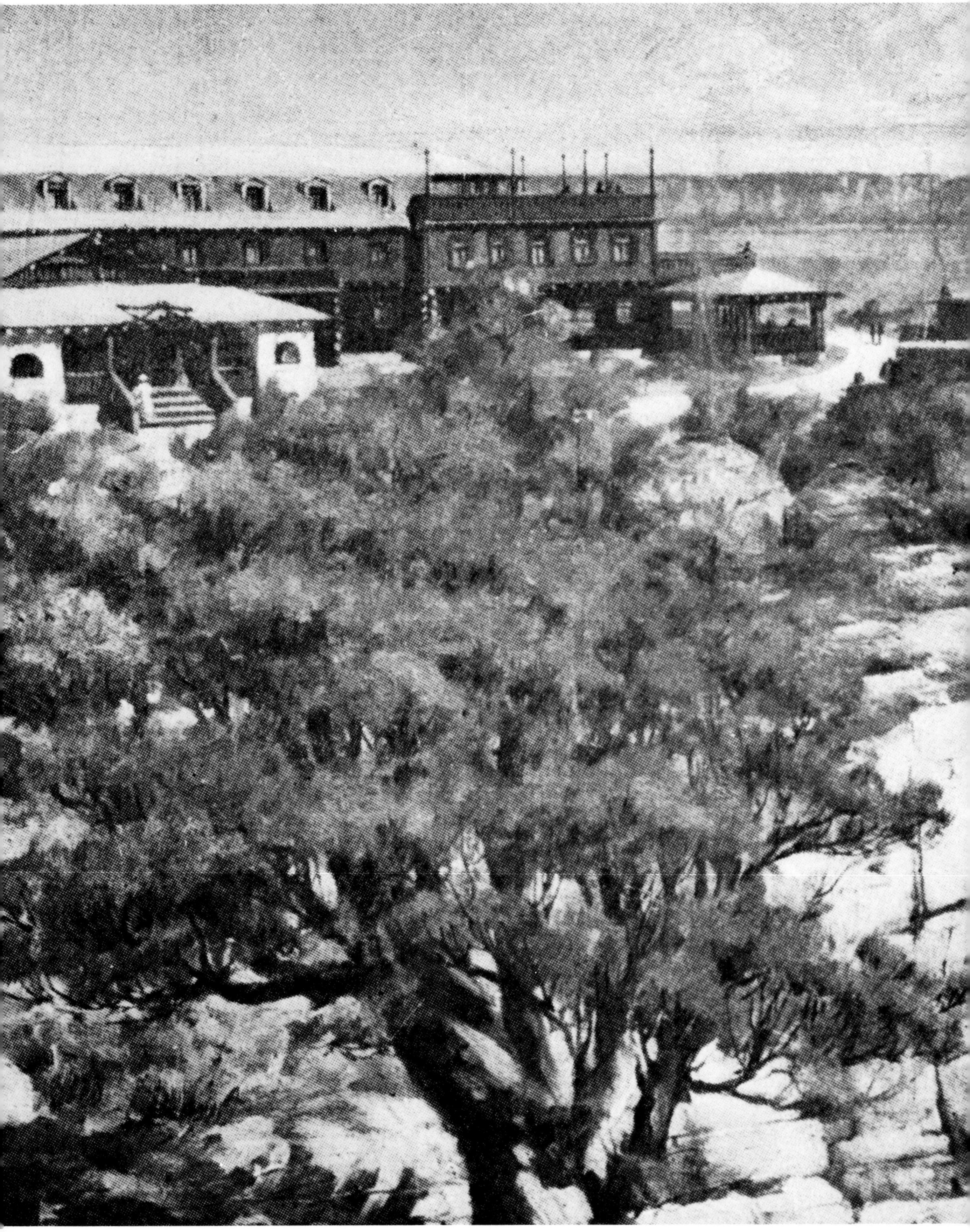

Above: The main entrance of the hotel in winter
Below: Ground-floor plan
Left: An artist's view of El Tovar

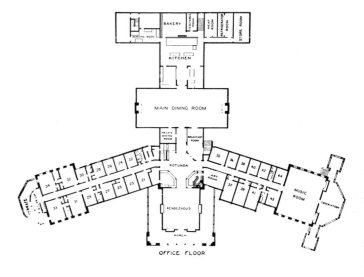

ALVARADO HOTEL

Albuquerque, New Mexico

The Alvarado Hotel was designed in 1901 by Charles F. Whittlesey of Chicago for the Santa Fe Railway, in a style meant to recall the missions of the Southwest. The complex included the hotel, the depot, a gift shop, and a restaurant, all organized around garden courtyards and linked by arcades. The rough stucco walls were unadorned, and decorative features were restricted to the parapets, towers, and entrances. The hotel was one of many throughout the Southwest managed by Fred Harvey and staffed by the Harvey girls, famous for their efficiency, courtesy, and neatly starched appearance.

The Alvarado served railroad passengers and local citizens until 1970, when, despite attempts to have it renovated as part of the downtown Albuquerque redevelopment plan, it was torn down and replaced by a parking lot.

YELLOWSTONE NATIONAL PARK

Wyoming

Yellowstone Park had been established thirty years before young Robert C. Reamer was hired by the Great Northern Railway to design tourist accommodations there in 1902. The buildings he created were largely responsible for establishing the rustic architectural idiom that was followed in the Western national parks through World War II.

Reamer's first hotel in the park was the Old Faithful Inn, built in 1902-1903. In 1913 and 1928 respectively, east and west wings were added, increasing its capacity to 500. Two factors determined the form and character of the hotel: the desire to make it compatible with the rustic setting and the need to make it adaptable to climatic extremes. The placement of the building on its site is indicative that nature is the primary attraction of the park. The façade was placed in a 90-degree relationship to the geyser so that visitors who timed their arrival correctly could view this natural wonder on their initial approach. There was a searchlight atop the building to chase away bears. This feature underscored the intimate relationship between the Old Faithful Inn and its surroundings.

The Inn rises like a small mountain of stacked logs, stone, and shingles. The great sweep of the central gabled roof recalls a number of images beloved by the Craftsman Movement. The great stone base, the piers of stacked logs, and the brackets of peeled branches all suggest the romantic notion of a frontiersman's cabin enlarged to gigantic proportions. As an observer commented in <u>Western Architect</u> magazine in 1904, the building was a product of the forest, built with ax, saw, and hammer and containing "not a yard of plaster." Even the interiors of the guest rooms and corridors are finished with peeled logs. The principal architectural feature is the huge pitched roof, punctuated by rows of dormer windows that appear to indicate the levels of interior stories but actually allow shafts of sunlight to penetrate the soaring lobby within. The interior of the lobby is dominated by a mammoth four-sided stone fireplace and by a maze of tree-branch balconies and catwalks that both awe and delight the visitor.

Reamer's second hotel was built near the Grand Canyon of the Yellowstone during the winter of 1910—1911. Workmen suffered through snow and sub-zero tempera-

The log piers and tree-branch brackets at the Old Faithful Inn suggest a woodsman's cabin on a fantastically grand scale.

The lobby at the Old Faithful Inn, dominated by a monumental stone fireplace and tree-branch balconies, is an architectural expression of surrounding nature.

tures to have the hotel ready for the summer season. Supposedly, the kitchen was completed first so that its ovens could be used for heating the nails to keep them from becoming brittle and breaking under the hammer.

The Canyon Hotel was beautifully placed on its hillside site. "I built it in keeping with the place where it stands," said Reamer. "Nobody could improve upon that. To be at discord with the landscape would be almost a crime. To try to improve upon it would be an impertinence." The hotel's main section contained the dining room, guest rooms, and services sheltered under a broad, dormer-covered hipped roof. A large central lounge was stepped forward of the main wing. In his travels to various American resorts, Reamer had discovered that guests tended to congregate in only some of the many rooms usually provided for reading, writing, and socializing. Accordingly, he decided to give the Canyon Hotel one large room to suit all these needs. A cascade of wide stairs made the entrance from the lobby particularly dramatic. A ceiling of beautiful wood trusses made art out of structure, while bays and furniture groupings defined specific areas within the space. The end of the room was almost entirely glazed and acted as a sun parlor.

As at Old Faithful, wood was the major building material used. But instead of the rustic logs and rough shingles of the earlier building, the Canyon Hotel was constructed of smoothly planed, carefully joined lumber. The architectural forms Reamer employed recall the work of members of Chicago's Prairie School or the wooden bungalows of West Coast architects like Charles and Henry Greene.

Robert Reamer's Yellowstone hotels served the park admirably until the 1960s, when a powerful earthquake damaged both of them. The Canyon Hotel was deemed a hazard and torn down. Although the Old Faithful Inn had been structurally weakened, it was repaired and is still in use.

Right: Couple enjoying the restful rusticity of their room in the Old Faithful Inn at the turn of the century
Left, above: The lounge at the Canyon Hotel
Left, center: The broad landing between the lobby and the lounge occasionally served as a stage for musical entertainment.
Left, below: Exterior of the Canyon Hotel, with the lounge projecting from the guest room wings

GLACIER NATIONAL PARK

Montana

Glacier Park encompasses some of the most moving and sublime scenery in America. High, rugged, snow-capped mountains rise precipitously out of clear blue lakes. To Easterners in search of an exotic West, this landscape suggested powerful images of Switzerland and Norway. The turn-of-the-century American tourist was often faced with incomparably magnificent scenery. In an effort to understand and assimilate these new landscapes, the tourist would usually compare them to others in more familiar places, especially in Europe. As an extension of this comparison, they expected the buildings in these landscapes to be designed in an equally evocative style. Thus the hotels in Glacier Park resembled great hand-hewn chalets.

The site of Lake McDonald Lodge was first settled by George Snyder, who, with Milo Apgar and Charlie Howe, built a small hotel there in 1895. Around 1905 John L. Lewis acquired the hotel and added new facilities, including guest cabins. When Glacier National Park was established in 1910, the Lewises were permitted to continue operating their hotel. During the winter of 1913—1914 a new Lewis Glacier Hotel was constructed to plans by architects Cutter and Malmgram of Spokane, Washington. The hotel, which survives today as Lake McDonald Lodge, has clapboard siding, hipped roofs with prominent brackets, and log railings, evoking the ambience of a Swiss alpine resort.

When the Great Northern Railway reached the entrance to Glacier Park, the decision was made to build a hotel to house the Easterners who would surely flock to see the scenery and to rough it in the wilderness. The Glacier Park Hotel, designed by Thomas D. McMahon of Saint Paul, Minnesota, opened on June 15, 1913. Local Indians promptly pinned on the behemoth the name "Oom-Coo-La-Mush-Taw," which means—we are told—"Big Tree Lodge." The appellation is entirely appropriate. The sixty tree trunks that support the building were brought to the site from Oregon and Washington. They were 36 to 42 inches in diameter and 40 feet long, and were from five hundred to eight hundred years old.

Lobby at the Glacier Park Hotel, dominated by rustic Ionic columns. Japanese lanterns introduce an Oriental theme.

Lakeside cottages provide an alternative to hotel accommodations at the Glacier.

The lobby of the hotel is one of the most astonishing spaces of this century. The great room is 60 feet tall and is dominated by two rows of the huge tree trunks, which support balconies overlooking the lobby floor. The top of each natural column is adorned with horizontal logs that suggest the volute scrolls of the classical Ionic order in a rustic guise. The use of rustic columns may have been inspired by a similar treatment in the Forestry Building at the Lewis and Clark Centennial Exposition in Portland, Oregon, a few years earlier. The counters and tables in the lobby are supported by sawn-off tree trunks, and all of the timbers in this remarkable room retain their bark. Around the walls is a frieze painted by Indians that depicts the history of the Blackfoot tribe.

The upper part of the dining-room wall is also ornamented by a frieze, depicting scenes from Glacier Park. Each image is separated from the next by a totem pole. Although natural and Indian themes predominate in the building, early visitors to the hotel may have been surprised to find their waitresses dressed in Swiss costume. The use of Chinese blue-willow-patterned table settings and the presence of a Japanese couple in their native costume wheeling a tea-and-coffee cart through the lobby may have been allusions to the proximity of the Pacific Coast to the Orient. These touches also reflected the interest in exotic cultures fashionable at the turn of the century. The easy blend of images in one building —here rustic, Alpine, and Oriental—is characteristically American.

In the early years of Glacier's operation, local Montanans were skeptical of the hotel's Eastern city-bred guests. The rustic elegance of the building and the elaborate garb of its clientele seemed at odds with the wildness of the surrounding park as well as with the tourists' alleged intentions to rough it. This apparent paradox was simply one more indication that this resort hotel was —as it remains—a special place that allowed an essentially urban clientele to assume the role of hardy outdoorsmen by day and of elegantly dressed gentlemen by night.

The automobile beneath the main entrance gate indicates the monumental scale of the place.

LOBBY, PARADISE INN, RAINIER NATIONAL PARK

Left: The lobby at the Paradise Inn at Mount Rainier National Park, Washington, is a restatement on a smaller scale of the rustic mode established at Yellowstone and Glacier. Above: The hotel's steep-pitched roof complements its mountain setting.

WHITE SULPHUR Springs

GREENBRIER COUNTY,

WEST VIRGINIA.

A. HOEN & CO., RICHMOND, VA.

THE GREENBRIER
White Sulphur Springs, West Virginia

The Greenbrier is the direct descendant of the Grand Central Hotel, known affectionately in its later years as the "Old White," which was built in 1858 to supplement the cottage colony at White Sulphur Springs. The hotel as it exists today is the product of many wings added over time, but the Greenbrier has maintained throughout the architectural vocabulary of the antebellum Southern mansion. Arcades below, a grand colonnade above, and large graceful temple porticoes, all in white, are the architectural elements suitable for a hotel intended to perpetuate the mythic life-style of the Old South, with its emphasis on gentility and impeccable manners. To stay at the Greenbrier is to immerse oneself in a latter-day aristocratic Southern atmosphere that is one of the few survivals of a legendary past.

In 1870, railroad connections to White Sulphur Springs made the spa accessible from all parts of the country. The Old White was no longer the exclusive domain of wealthy Southerners, even though it remained the most visible symbol of the Old South. In 1910 the hotel was purchased by the Chesapeake and Ohio Railway Company. Frederick Junius Sterner was hired to design the Greenbrier, a seven-story, 250-room structure, adjacent to the dilapidated Grand Central. Frederick Sterry, former manager of the Plaza Hotel in New York City, came to White Sulphur Springs, bringing with him a new clientele. A different type of guest began to patronize the Old White, one who frequently arrived in his own railroad car. For the less affluent visitor, a private car could be rented for $800 to permit a stylish arrival. Noted guests of the 1910s included the Vanderbilts, the Armours, Woodrow Wilson, and Edward, Prince of Wales. Not even the austerity of World War I dampened the Greenbrier's atmosphere.

The resort was once again enlarged during the prosperous 1920s, but the Old White had become increasingly run down. In 1922, it failed to pass the state fire inspection and was demolished. (In the years preceding its destruction, the lobby had been misused as a golf practice range.) Even the newer Greenbrier was not making money for its owners, but its role as a corporate entertainment spot more than made up for the Chesapeake and Ohio's losses. After the Crash of 1929, the complex was further enlarged and improved, and the hotel flourished during the

This nineteenth-century brochure conveys the mood of quiet gentility at White Sulphur Springs.

Depression. Families that had formerly maintained great estates in various regions found it more economical to live for a season at a hotel like the Greenbrier.

During the winter of 1941-1942 the Greenbrier housed enemy diplomats, who spent lavishly at its shops. Later in 1942, architects Small, Smith and Reeb were hired to transform the hotel into a 2,200-bed army hospital. The existing furniture was either auctioned off or burned. After serving as the Ashford General Hospital, the structure was repurchased by the Chesapeake and Ohio in 1947, and Small, Smith and Reeb returned to change the military hospital back into a civilian hotel. Dorothy Draper decorated all the interiors, featuring her distinctive floral wallpapers and fabrics, many of them designed especially for the hotel. No two bedrooms were decorated exactly alike. Some of the grand public spaces of the original building were remodeled to give them a more modern, intimate character. The Greenbrier still draws the wealthy and famous as it seeks to keep up with the times while preserving the ambience of the Old South that is its chief attraction.

Above: The pavilion above the spring itself is topped by a statue of Hygeia, the Greek goddess of health.
Right: Aerial view of the Greenbrier in the 1930s

THE ANTLERS

Colorado Springs, Colorado

General William Jackson Palmer, organizer of the Denver and Rio Grande Railroad, laid out Manitou Springs in the mountains above his new town at Colorado Springs in 1871, in the hope that it would become a first-class spa comparable to resorts in the East. Manitou did become fashionable, and visitors reported a social whirl and an elaborate spectacle that rivaled glittering Saratoga. But Colorado Springs itself proved more attractive to aristocratic settlers than did Manitou. The presence of a large English colony soon gave the town the nickname "Little London." As the number of demanding visitors increased, it became clear that Colorado Springs needed a first-class hotel.

General Palmer, as the developer of the town, agreed to build a luxury resort hotel in a four-acre park adjacent to his railroad depot. Peabody and Stearns of Boston designed the building in the Queen Anne Style with lower walls of stone, upper floors clad in shingles, and the characteristic turrets, gables, and dormer windows. One of the directors of the enterprise was a local doctor with novel notions about good ventilation and sanitary plumbing. The hotel therefore incorporated a stack ventilation system that drew all harmful vapors from the bathrooms and out through ventilators on the roof, where they were expelled into the fresh mountain air. As promotional brochures proclaimed, "no stationary wash stands are allowed in the chambers, so that the travelled guest will not need to use the cork he no doubt carried and which he so often must use to stop up the death-dealing waste pipe."

The Antlers, so called because of the many trophy heads that adorned the lobby, opened in 1882. Its elegance and excellent cuisine soon pulled it through an initial period of economic trouble and established it as the foremost resort hotel in the Pike's Peak region. In 1898, at the height of its popularity, the Antlers was destroyed by fire. General Palmer promised the people of Colorado Springs that he would build an even grander Antlers on the same spot. Six architectural firms were asked to submit plans, and the award went to Varien and Sterner, a large office from New York City.

The new Antlers was in the Italian Renaissance Revival Style and was constructed of cream-colored brick with white stone trim and a red tile roof. The twin-

The first Antlers Hotel, designed by Peabody and Stearns of Boston, brought Eastern fashion to the Rocky Mountains.

towered structure stood five stories tall on the entrance side and seven stories on the rear, the downhill side facing the park. So-called Florentine balconies and green-and-white awnings graced its windows, while its grand piazza, loggias, and terraces opened on spectacular views of the gardens and the Rocky Mountains.

The interior of the new building was as impressive as its exterior. In addition to 236 guest rooms, all with temperature controls and telephones and many with private baths, there were public rooms of every size and for every purpose. Marble fireplaces and stairs, Roman mosaic floors, Flemish oak beams, sparkling crystal chandeliers, and costly hangings assured the public that no expense had been spared to create an atmosphere of cosmopolitan elegance.

The new Antlers opened in 1901, delighting both locals and visitors. An early brochure was openly snobbish: "The Antlers does not cater to cheap patronage and its prices are sufficiently high to insure the best quality of everything." The hotel offered the usual aristocratic pastimes of automobiling, golf, tennis, polo, cricket, and croquet. Trapshooting, lawn bowling, and mountain climbing were popular, as was riding to hounds with jack rabbits and coyotes standing in for foxes. The hotel's charms attracted socialites, mining magnates, and even presidents, such as Teddy Roosevelt. While a guest, Katharine Lee Bates composed "America the Beautiful" after an apparently inspirational excursion to the top of Pike's Peak.

The Antlers began to feel the pinch of competition after the opening of the Broadmoor in 1918, though it held its own until World War II. Extensive renovations and a change of ownership in the 1950s failed to sustain its fading popularity. Finally, in 1964, the Antlers was torn down to make way for a shopping center, an office complex, and a high-rise motor hotel that now carries the name, if not the traditions and spirit, of what had been hailed as "the best hotel in the West."

Left, above: The formal furnishings of guest rooms in the second Antlers contrast with the hotel's rugged setting.
Far left, below: Façade of the second Antlers   Left, below: Engraved view of the first Antlers Hotel

HOTEL COLORADO

Glenwood Springs, Colorado

Captain Isaac Cooper recognized opportunity when he saw it. The bubbling hot springs that he discovered along the banks of the Colorado River had the potential for becoming a grand and lucrative spa. But Cooper's ambitions for his springs were hampered by his lack of capital. When the Denver and Rio Grande Railroad reached the tiny town of Glenwood in 1887, the bathhouses were, as Earl Pomeroy notes, little more than crude sheds with "tubs no more than holes excavated with a shovel and rented for 15 cents a customer." Aspen silver king Walter Devereaux became interested in the springs and diverted the course of the river around the source, in order to expose them. In 1888, he constructed an elaborate two-story, 42-room bathhouse and a swimming pool 500 feet long—the largest hot-mineral-water pool in the world. Five years later, the Hotel Colorado was built on the hill above the pool at a cost of $850,000. Its architects, Boring, Tilton and Mellon of New York, modeled the new hotel after the Villa Medici in Rome. The building enclosed three sides of a large terraced garden court containing a deep trout-stocked pool and a fountain that shot a jet of water 100 feet into the air. The Italian Renaissance Revival Style was well suited for the decoration of what is, in fact, a very simple box-like building. Red sandstone and cream brick walls and red roofs harmonized with the colors of the surrounding mountains.

Inside the hotel, the public rooms opened off a long central lobby. Several hundred guests could enjoy the hotel's excellent cuisine in the 5,000-square-foot dining room, provided they dressed in the requisite formal attire. The ballroom boasted a maple floor "as smooth as glass." Upstairs were 200 bedrooms, nearly half with private baths and most with fireplaces and brass bedsteads.

From its opening, the Hotel Colorado was one of the most snobbish resorts in the state. Formal dress codes and high prices discouraged the local residents, predominantly rough-and-ready miners, from ever entering the building. Walter

The dining room at the Hotel Colorado boasts a waterfall, which is intended to suggest a mountain stream.

Raymond was the manager, and the staff was trained in Boston. Although the hotel drew a steady stream of Raymond and Whitcomb tourists who stopped over for a few days, most of its guests stayed a good part of the summer season, whiling away their time in the pool, hunting, fishing, or playing polo. Magnates like J. P. Armour of Chicago and characters like Buffalo Bill Cody, Diamond Jim Brady, and the unsinkable Molly Brown all found their way to Glenwood Springs. The Hotel Colorado was a favorite haunt of that irrepressible patron of resorts, Theodore Roosevelt. The president and his large entourage would hunt in the mountains during the day and return to the hotel for glittering banquets in the evening—roughing it in style. Many of Teddy's companions were hardly well versed in the social graces. At dinner one evening the president noticed several of his guides puzzling over which of the many pieces of silver to use. "Grab the implement nearest you, boys!" he shouted, in good-natured encouragement.

Changing resort patterns in the 1910s and 1920s dealt harshly with the Hotel Colorado. The number of seasonal guests declined. The cancellation of railroad resort runs made the hotel much less accessible. The army of Boston servants were the first amenity to be curtailed as the atmosphere of the place assumed a much more informal quality. In recent years, the Hotel Colorado has found renewed life as a regional playground for nearby Denver.

The Colorado River flows past the Hotel Colorado (left) and its bathhouse and pool (right).

ATLANTIC CITY
New Jersey

In 1845, Dr. Jonathon R. Pitney visited a barren stretch of the New Jersey coast and envisioned a second Cape May. He persuaded some Philadelphians to invest in his vision, and in 1854, with rail service between Philadelphia and Atlantic City established, the town's first boom began. Although hotels and private villas were constructed almost immediately, for several decades the new resort was secondary to Cape May, Long Branch, and other points along the Jersey shore.

In the 1890s, as neighboring vacation spots declined, Atlantic City blossomed and soon deserved the title "America's Playground—the Mecca of Millions." The publicity event that placed it before the national eye and has kept it there ever since is the Miss America beauty contest, first held in 1921. Although it boasted of being the place for the elite, the resort always attracted a socially diverse crowd —so diverse, in fact, that most of its visitors were from Philadelphia's working classes, drawn there by the beach and amusements similar to those of Coney Island. The boardwalk and piers were alive with the excitement of music and dancing, fireworks, stunts, carnival shows, and souvenir shops. The Philadelphia newspapers were fond of exposing the presence as well of numerous dens of iniquity and prostitution, but this was a problem hardly unique to this resort. Atlantic City also attracted the successful business and professional classes and the nouveaux riches, who frequented the large hotels that loomed up like a vast wall along the beach.

In 1902, fire destroyed many of these early hotels. The ornate wooden structures were quickly replaced with a number of pacesetting buildings that radically changed Atlantic City's skyline. Here, as at no other resort of that time, the site was urban in character. Land costs along the beach were very high, which forced hotels to be built as thin vertical slabs stretching back from a narrow boardwalk frontage. A grandiose entry on the boardwalk itself was very desirable, and the high rents that could be obtained for shop space led many hotels to build long commercial arcades connecting the beach with the lobby in the center of the building. Above these arcades, removed from the crowds, terraces overlooking the ocean were provided for dining and taking the sea air.

This engraved view of Atlantic City illustrates all of its nineteenth-century attractions: hotels, the boardwalk, the surf, and socializing on the veranda.

The wave of rebuilding coincided with improved means of fire-proof construction utilizing a concrete frame with masonry or terra-cotta cladding. The new Marlborough-Blenheim Hotel of 1906 was hailed by architectural critics as a pioneer effort in the aesthetic treatment of concrete. Its architects, Price and McLanahan of Philadelphia, took advantage of the material's malleability to create domes, undulating facades, and sculptured ornament. Instead of imitating traditional architectural details, they devised a new iconography. Shells, mermaids, seaweed, and other ocean forms in baroque profusion were modeled out of tile and terra cotta, relating the building symbolically to its shore site.

The Hotel Traymore of 1907 was also designed by Price and McLanahan, using a similar concrete structural system clad with stone, brick, and terra cotta. These architects were known for their dramatic and inventive interiors. In the Traymore's famous Submarine Bar, a fish-tank skylight cast rippling shadows over the floor and walls.

Atlantic City reached the height of its popularity in the 1920s. The Depression only hastened its decline from fashion, as improved transportation and competition lured its flush patronage away. By the early 1970s, the resort was run down. Many of the hotels suffered from chronic financial difficulties and ill repair. Both the Traymore and the Marlborough-Blenheim were judged to be white elephants and dynamited.

Aging buildings have cast a pall upon Atlantic City, although promises of rejuvenation are alive in the wake of legalized gambling. The city's promoters feel the resort could be the Eastern counterpart of Las Vegas. Revival will depend upon the developers' ability to erase its decrepit image and do away with reminders of its tawdry past. Yet it seems unlikely that Atlantic City, robbed of any atmosphere it once had, will ever again cater to a wealthy, trendy crowd. Unlike Las Vegas, which will always benefit from its bizarre and unlikely location in the desert, Atlantic City now seems too ordinary, set in too familiar a landscape. It will take a new and unique architectural image to transform the resort into something truly new and fresh.

The Marlborough-Blenheim Hotel cast an animated silhouette against the sky, heightening its image as an exotic seaside place.

Between the World Wars

President Woodrow Wilson had hoped that the triumph of the Allies in World War I would place the United States in a position of world leadership, spreading American democratic ideals around the globe. But the American people, horrified by the war and disgusted with the "ungrateful and duplicitous" Europeans, sought only to protect their heritage from contamination. Most of them resolutely turned their backs on things European, searching instead for a way to recapture the good old days—an attitude beautifully encapsulated in Warren Harding's catchphrase "Return to Normalcy." Yet America of the postwar era was a different world from prewar America. Mass communication—radio, movies, and publications—blurred class distinctions and gave Americans common assumptions about speech, dress, behavior, and idealized images of the good life. Even though large social and ethnic divisions remained, many social restrictions began to break down, and the aspirations of an extremely broad middle class became standards of American taste.

The United States emerged from World War I intact, industrially well organized, and richer than ever before. With the new prosperity came a wave of optimism. Jazz music, the Charleston, numerous fads, and a tremendous building boom all symbolized the frenzied pace of the 1920s. After the belt-tightening war years, Americans were ready to devote a great deal of money and energy to having a good time. As in earlier decades, the large resort hotel offered a place for recreation and for getting away from the pressures of daily life, as well as an opportunity for social and business contacts. But in the 1920s, more people than ever before were able to afford the luxury of a vacation. More and more, the vacation became associated with the greatly increased mobility afforded by the automobile.

Just as the railroad had once affected the patterns of resort life, the automobile now began to exert a tremendous influence on resort development. The unprecedented mobility it afforded meant that any site with some natural interest had potential as a resort. In contrast to the more structured pattern of the railroad, the lure and the freedom of the highway encouraged tourists to travel from place to place, often stopping for only a night or two at any one hotel. Resorts now had to accommodate these transient guests as well as those more traditional resorters who stayed for longer periods of time. New hotels were located on primary highways, while many older hotels were bypassed by improved roads and consequently ignored by travelers.

Although prosperity and widespread auto ownership furthered the democratization of the vacation, just as the excursion trains to places like Coney Island and Atlantic City had in the late 1880s and 1890s, the grand resort hotel remained largely the province of the well-to-do. High prices allowed the older established resorts and some of the ritzier newcomers to maintain the exclusive atmosphere their patrons desired. Less affluent tourists enjoyed their vacations at more modest hotels, automobile camps, and roadside cabins.

The 1920s were boom years for the hotel industry. Tales of aged railroad employees, former hot-dog vendors, or one-time bicycle racers making millions overnight in real estate speculation were a staple of the popular magazines. Optimism and prosperity combined to encourage elaborate investment schemes and building booms all across the country. "Join the cream of society at the new American Mediterranean"—"Explore the wonders of our unspoiled mountain scenery"—"Marvel at the rugged grandeur of the West." As usual, the grand resort hotel often served

as the social core and established the architectural character of a real estate development or promotional scheme. The Cloister Inn at Boca Raton, Florida, the Santa Barbara Biltmore, and the Arizona Biltmore at Phoenix were all surrounded by luxurious new vacation and retirement homes. Many of the mountain resorts, unable to match the sunny climates of their tropical winter competitors, sought to popularize winter sports such as skiing and tobogganing. Prosperity also encouraged established resorts to rehabilitate or replace older buildings and expand their facilities. The Homestead in Hot Springs, Virginia, added a high-rise tower atop its red brick Georgian-styled building from the 1910s, which in turn had replaced a venerable nineteenth-century structure.

Not all of the boom hotels were successful, architecturally or economically. Many had been inefficiently planned and poorly built in the rush to lure investors, and as real estate activity declined it was discovered that their location and facilities were inadequate to sustain tourist interest. Others, like the Hotel Rolyat in Saint Petersburg, Florida, were beautifully designed and well built, but nevertheless succumbed to financial collapse when the boom bubble burst.

Corporate ownership and hotel chains came to dominate the hotel industry during the 1920s. Every aspect of hotel operation was placed in the hands of professional managers, who were often graduates of hotel schools such as that established at Cornell University in the early 1920s. Architects and interior decorators specialized in hotel design and furnishing, while experts in kitchen and laundry facilities planned efficient services. Sharp-eyed accountants and financial consultants looked after hotels' finances. The number of individual resort owners dwindled as professionalism and corporate ownership became the keys to successful hotel operation. The problems that hotel managers faced were more complex and vexing than they had been in the previous century. Prohibition, for example, created severe financial stress by eliminating a major source of income and entertainment. Managers made the best of the situation by emphasizing excellent personal service and by devising a host of new entertainments.

While professional training and specialization improved hotel standards of comfort and efficiency, such changes also narrowed the range of architectural possibilities that were considered workable. Consequently, hotel design in the 1920s followed a few proven directions, with occasional improvements in detail. Guest rooms and public spaces were placed in a standardized relation to one another. Circulation patterns and views of the site were accommodated without sacrificing the logic and economy of the structural and mechanical systems. Fireproof construction of steel and concrete with masonry infill was now the rule.

With the exception of hotels in resort cities like Atlantic City and Miami Beach, where land costs dictated high-rise solutions, resorts were free from the constraints of an urban site. They generally expanded outward rather than upward. Public rooms could be developed independently with little concentration of volume around elevators. Service areas were invariably hidden from the guests' view so that the character of the site and the mood of the interior spaces would not be marred.

No single architectural style dominated this era, and many were easily permitted by the standardized organization of the building. Although architects were well aware of the importance of character, most architectural elements were regarded as applied decoration, and often these visible details were fully developed only after the major decisions regarding the over-all organization had been reached. Hotel architect Leonard Schultze expresses the attitudes that prevailed in the 1920s:

It is impossible to say that Italian renaissance, Gothic, Louis XVI or any other period of architecture is best adapted for any particular type of hotel. The exterior of any American steel-frame building is so vastly different from that of the buildings of the older countries where established styles of architecture prevail that no matter what particular type of architecture is employed the result will be only one of decoration.... It is necessary to subordinate and at times sacrifice what the designer frequently considers his individual tastes and desires in order to provide adequately for the commercial uses and requirements of the buildings. He has no right to indulge his fancy in over-decoration, or in the use of more expensive materials for decoration than may be deemed essential—necessary to make the building a safe commercial investment. Hotels are planned and erected, except in a few and rare cases, with the primary idea of making money; in addition they are expected to supply the needs of the public, and at the same time afford the greatest number of conveniences possible.

Efficiency and economy may have been emphasized in design discussions, but the value of a distinctive architectural style was also recognized. An architectural setting that would prove attractive to guests, hold their interest during their stay, and inspire them to return was justified as good advertising and good business. According to John Bowman of the Bowman-Biltmore chain:

From the very inception of the hotel project to the development of its most recent innovation an almost primary demand is made upon architecture. Fine motor cars stop at fine entrances; social functions need impressive settings; discrimination calls for good taste. In varying degrees the modern hotel demands atmosphere, which fundamentally is an appeal to the senses. Color and texture, mass and proportion skillfully disposed in a series of connotations—this is architecture,

Above: La Valencia Hotel in La Jolla embodies the Mediterranean ambience selected by Southern California's promoters in the 1920s.
Below: A tea dance in the Oriental Tea Garden at the Flamingo Hotel in Miami Beach

and the true background without which the finest service would be little appreciated by the American public.

The demand for distinctive and even romantic architectural settings led resort hotel owners of the 1920s to build in styles that involved a relevant theme drawn from local history, idyllic scenery, or climate. The use of Mediterranean motifs in Florida or of Spanish imagery in California and the Southwest are examples of historical association, however ephemeral or legendary, exploited to create a memorable atmosphere. Rustic, picturesque, irregular architectural styles remained popular in wilderness settings, even though achieving that character in a building best described as a small city was no easy task. The Ahwahnee in Yosemite National Park is an example—a steel and concrete structure successfully disguised as a rustic lodge constructed of boulders and wood.

There was a great range in the degree of accuracy with which historical models were followed. At the Breakers hotel in Palm Beach, architects Schultze and Weaver displayed an almost archaeological concern with correctness; specific Italian villas served as sources both for the public rooms and for the over-all scheme. Most hotels were not so closely tied to a model and relied upon precedent only for scale, massing, and detail. This second approach allowed the architect to embrace simple, modern, and much more economical building forms without discarding connections with the past altogether. Many architects and hotel operators feared that their hotels would be stark, barren, and uninviting if all the familiar ornamental elements of traditional architecture were eliminated. Through a process of simplification of historical forms, architects created buildings that seemed at once contemporary and traditional; the Santa Barbara Biltmore is an example of a hotel designed in this manner. By the end of the 1920s, however, designers began to question the appropriateness of using historical models for buildings that functioned in a decidedly modern way. Influenced by the philosophy of modern European architecture, some hotel architects chose to strip away ornament entirely both for the purposes of economy and to present a sleek modern image.

Hotel men viewed interior decoration as the most important factor in creating mood. A professional decorator was usually hired to complement the architect's skills. The people who visited resorts were accustomed to antiques and art objects tastefully arranged in their own homes, and they expected the same or better from resort interiors. A consistent feature of resort hotels in the 1920s was the careful treatment of materials. Marble, tiles, exquisite woods, and textiles were employed with great finesse and craftsmanship to achieve beautiful effects and to create a level of lavish splendor that surpassed most domestic settings.

Although the exterior architectural style or character often set the tone for interior decoration, rooms on individual themes were included to give variety. Certain public rooms acquired almost stereotypical characteristics: the lobby was stately and subdued, perhaps in an Italian Renaissance style; the dining room was at once elegant and novel, possibly patterned after a room in Versailles; a Tahitian terrace or a Spanish patio added a touch of the exotic; and a dark, wood-paneled Olde English Bar and Grill provided a proper masculine retreat for the gentlemen. The sophistication and luxury of resort life were reflected in the surroundings; it was felt to be particularly important that the character of the interior be compatible with the clientele. An overly formal interior might make guests feel ill-at-ease, inconsistent with the purpose of a vacation as a time for relaxation and feeling at one's best; an excessively casual setting presented its own problems.

By the late 1920s, interior designers faced the same dilemma as architects. The pressures of modernism were met by a resistance to throwing out familiar, traditional architectural forms. Henry J. B. Hoskins, a member of the architectural firm of Holabird and Root, made these observations in 1929:

As people generally sought in the hotel something which their own homes lacked, it was rather natural that they should be impressed with the lavishly carved and embellished designs of the period styles, with the growing accumulation of objects of art, and an extravagance of decorative effect suggestive of commercial prosperity and advancement. But with the development of a more democratic taste the desire for regal expenditure and lavishness has diminished to a large extent in favor of simplicity and refinement.

The atmosphere of the period styles has given way to a studied attempt to express ourselves in our own way and to create a suitable setting for the life of our own time. The "modern" trend in design is toward simple severity with the use of flat planes, light and shadow, of clean-cut angles and flutings and sharp color contrasts arranged with the same rhythm as modern dancing and music, and with the same simplicity and directness as the sweeping lines of our automobiles and airplanes. Careful selection, discrimination, and the elimination of non-essentials form the basis of modern decoration. Furniture is slowly conforming to the same idea and is being designed in harmony with the decorative scheme with strong lines, flat surfaces and a tendency toward affording ease as well as giving architectural effect.

In 1929, the Architectural Forum expressed the proud conviction that aside from such superficial matters as styling, the art of hotel design had reached a state of near-perfection, and indeed there was some justification for this belief. Hotel services and operations were standardized and mechanized to a high degree of sophistication, and no new gadgets were on the immediate horizon. Television, although anticipated,

THE *Surfcomber*

NEW Miami Beach Hotel

DIRECTLY ON THE OCEAN AT 17TH STREET
Near Lincoln Road

**150 FEET OF PRIVATE BEACH
SWIMMING POOL
TROPICAL PATIO
COCKTAIL LOUNGE
COFFEE SHOP**
all Outside Rooms
OWNERSHIP MANAGEMENT

**FULLY AIR CONDITIONED
STEAM HEATED**

OPEN ALL YEAR

Above: The Hollywood Beach Hotel in Florida exhibits the classic combination of a luxurious hotel building with elaborate formal gardens.
Right: Hotel advertisements of the 1930s reflected the stream-lined forms of modern hotel architecture.

was still at least two decades away from widespread use.

The confidence expressed by hotel men was severely shaken by the Depression. Investment capital was gone; resort construction halted. The scarcity of funds for travel and recreation severely reduced business in even the most established hotels. Railroad excursion runs became unprofitable and were drastically curtailed, leaving many older resorts virtually isolated. Hotels of all kinds, and resort hotels in particular, had to find ways to survive financially. Some lowered their rates and eliminated some of their trappings to attract a broader and more informal clientele. The Royal Poinciana and the Breakers, for example, announced their rates in promotional brochures for the first time. Many hotels began grudgingly to cater to conventions and other groups.

Despite valiant attempts to attract business during the Depression, many hotels went into receivership; some were torn down. Neglected buildings generated problems that extended beyond the Depression itself. Hotels that were left unused often decayed so badly that even when business picked up again, renovation costs were prohibitively expensive. Some, like the Tampa Bay and later the Ponce de Leon, were saved from destruction by conversion to new uses. A few of the most fashionable resorts managed to do a respectable business even during the Depression years. The Greenbrier became a more economical substitute for its patrons expensive vacation homes. The Hotel Del Coronado, benefitting from its proximity to San Diego and Los Angeles, enjoyed the reputation of being a favored playground of the glamorous and prosperous Hollywood movie colony.

One of many cool, covered walkways at the Cloister Inn, Boca Raton

THE BROADMOOR

Colorado Springs, Colorado

It is difficult to believe that the fabulous Broadmoor Hotel never yielded a good financial return to its builder, but then multimillionaire Spencer Penrose didn't seem to care. Just owning a popular hotel was reward enough during the booming 1920s, although he once remarked that he thought the Broadmoor was "a monument to a damned fool."

The hotel was not the first losing enterprise on the site. In 1891, Silesian Count James de Pourtalès had constructed a Georgian-styled casino there, hoping to make enough money from the sale of spirits and entertainment to visitors from nearby "dry" Colorado Springs to refurbish his ancestral home. The casino was quite popular, but expenses outstripped profits. Attempts at publicity ended in fiascos: a lady balloonist who was hired to parachute into the grounds landed in the artificial lake and nearly drowned before she could be hauled to shore. Finally the count gave up and headed to Arizona in search of gold. This time luck smiled on him. He returned to Silesia a wealthy man.

The count's Broadmoor casino and properties were never reclaimed, however, and remained in receivership until mining and real estate magnate Spencer Penrose bought them in 1916. The well-traveled and flamboyant Penrose had long enjoyed the life in fine hotels. After locking horns with the managers of the Antlers for allegedly riding his horse into the bar, he decided to put the place in the shade by building a luxury hotel of his own. With the aid of business associate Charles Tutt, Penrose began the monumental undertaking.

Architect Frederick Junius Sterner of New York, who had designed the nearby Antlers and the Greenbrier at White Sulphur Springs, was retained to convert his client's complex notions into a workable plan. Penrose wanted the outside of the building to be of pink terra cotta, the guest rooms to suggest Honolulu and Lausanne, and the ballroom to capture the atmosphere of the royal palace at Peking. Undaunted, Sterner inspected the site and decided instead that the hotel should be an "Italian" structure of pinkish stucco facing the mountains across the existing lake. His plans were judged too elaborate, and he was replaced by Warren and Wetmore, designers of such well-known buildings as the Biltmore and Ritz-Carlton

The Broadmoor's dining room staff, immaculately groomed and turned out, await the hotel's equally formal patrons.

Above: A mustachioed Spencer Penrose at the left poses with a celebrity guest, fighter Jack Dempsey (center). Left: Behind the scenes at the Broadmoor, all splendor and display are sacrificed for efficiency.

hotels and Grand Central Terminal, all in New York. They retained Sterner's image of an Italian palazzo while designing a much more economical structure. Construction began in 1917, despite the wartime shortage of labor and building materials.

Nothing could be done quickly enough or well enough to satisfy Penrose, who insisted on taking part in every decision, right down to selecting the bathroom fixtures. He also exercised his right to change his mind. Despite frequent arguments, the hotel and its grounds were completed in a remarkably brief time, and the Broadmoor opened in June 1918.

The Broadmoor is a compact nine-story building of steel frame and concrete block construction clad with stucco painted a soft color known as "Broadmoor pink." The true nature of the structural system is visible only in behind-the-scenes, functional spaces like the kitchen. The grand public rooms were originally decorated with elaborate plasterwork and frescoes and lavish period detailing that provided an elegant setting. The lobby was graced by a sweeping marble staircase. The dining rooms had plaster ceilings patterned to resemble latticework and painted in tones of old ivory and Wedgwood blue. The Georgian ballroom boasted marble pilasters, crystal chandeliers, and plum-colored hangings. An enclosed terrace faced the lake, and beyond lay an open-air plaza where guests could dine under the stars. The bedrooms all had private baths; many had sleeping porches. The main building was furnished with many fine antiques and works of art gathered by Mr. and Mrs. Penrose during their travels. The golf course, bridle paths, polo fields, tennis and squash courts, and the largest indoor swimming pool in the West were ready for the guests' enjoyment. The vast power and refrigeration plants, gardens, greenhouses, and livestock that enabled the hotel to function with apparent ease were, of course, kept out of sight.

A thousand select friends attended the splendid supper and festivities at Penrose's preview party. Unfortunately, the guest of honor, John D. Rockefeller, came down with a headache from the smell of fresh paint and went to the Antlers to get a good night's sleep.

During its first years, the Broadmoor was a busy place. Dances, parties, and sporting events of all sorts filled its schedule. Penrose had a real flair for grandiose publicity stunts and delighted in staging lavish entertainments. At one point, the Broadmoor played host to Jack Dempsey while he was training for his fight with Gene Tunney. The boxer put up with publicity photos and exhibition bouts in the ballroom until he was almost exhausted. He finally had to finish his training elsewhere.

Penrose's menagerie of rare animals was moved from his ranch to the hotel's new Cheyenne Mountain Zoo. He built an indoor polo field, a stadium, and miles of roads, including one to the top of Pike's Peak and one that ran from his hotel to his zoo and beyond to the top of nearby Cheyenne Mountain.

Only one cloud cast a shadow on these happy years for Penrose: Prohibition. It was not just that it reduced his profits; it infuriated him not to be able to buy a drink. When the Eighteenth Amendment took effect in 1919, he had the Broadmoor's entire $250,000 liquor supply moved into hiding at his club in New York, at his brother's home, in his own basement, and at several warehouses. He continued to enjoy his private stock and to flaunt his contempt for the law by displaying his empties in the hotel lobby. Repeal was one of his few bright moments of the Depression years. Two freight cars of "the goods" were removed from hiding and triumphantly returned to their place in the Broadmoor cellars. Not surprisingly, this excellent stock contributed to the appeal of the hotel during the years of World War II, when only poor-quality domestic spirits were available elsewhere.

Spencer Penrose did not live to see his hotel become popular with the military brass and America's elite during the Second World War, or its later financial success and expansion under the management of Charles Tutt and his sons. Penrose died of cancer in 1939 and was buried, as he wished, in a crypt near the large tower on Cheyenne Mountain that he had built as a monument to himself during the early 1930s. When friends pointed out that few people were likely to be interested in visiting the shrine of someone they had never heard of, Penrose had graciously dedicated the tower to the memory of his late friend Will Rogers. From up there on the mountain one overlooks the true Penrose memorial: the 5,000-acre, multi-million-dollar Broadmoor.

The original Broadmoor (right) and one of several later additions

THE BREAKERS

Palm Beach, Florida

During its peak years around the turn of the century, the Royal Poinciana was unable to accommodate all those who wanted to stay there. People were known to wait at other hotels along the coast until a room became available. Consequently, the Flagler system built the Palm Beach Inn on the ocean side of Palm Beach in 1895 to absorb the overflow from the older hotel. Although it was regarded as inferior socially, the Inn did have a splendid view of the ocean, and it was only a short ride by horsecar or Afromobile from the fancy doings of its neighbor. Additions were made soon after it was built, and the name was changed to "The Breakers." This wooden structure was destroyed in a spectacular fire in 1903. A second Breakers was built in 1906, but it too burned, in 1925, and was replaced by the current hotel, which opened on December 29, 1926.

The architectural firm of Schultze and Weaver of New York was chosen to design the third Breakers and to supervise the interior decoration and landscaping. They also prepared a plan, which was never executed, for a cottage community adjacent to the hotel. Schultze claimed that a memory of the Villa Medici in Rome inspired his design. Although the roughly H-shaped plan and two towers do suggest the sixteenth-century structure, that is about as far as the similarity goes. Structurally and functionally, the hotel is wholly modern. It is built of steel and reinforced concrete. The surface of the building is rough-textured buff stucco with concrete ornament of a darker color. The combination of stucco and stone with green window casings and sashes and a red tile roof successfully creates the Mediterranean architectural character and ambience that seemed appropriate to Florida in the 1920s.

The interiors, too, were based on elaborate historical precedent. Specific rooms in Italian villas and palaces served as models to be faithfully re-created or lovingly interpreted. Marble floors, travertine walls, rich molded-stucco sculptural details, and frescoes gave the vast dining room and lobby an air of magnificence that even its contemporaries were hard pressed to match.

The vast lobby of the Breakers is ornamented with motifs borrowed from Italian villas.

CLOISTER INN
Boca Raton, Florida

The town of Boca Raton was laid out in 1897 along the route of the Florida East Coast Railway. For the next quarter-century it was the domain of pineapple growers and vegetable farmers, who took advantage of its rich soil and good climate to make the place a center for the shipping of winter vegetables. The Florida land boom of 1924 and 1925 changed all that. The grandiose schemes of architect Addison Mizner and the even more fantastic promotions of his brother Wilson and advertising genius Harry Reichenbach transformed the sleepy little town into one of the most exclusive and expensive subdivisions in the nation. The Cloister Inn is the centerpiece of that development.

Addison Mizner had earned quite a reputation as architect to the social elite of Palm Beach. His own version of Spanish Renaissance architecture had made that Florida vacation spot one of the architectural wonders of America. When the boom began he, like so many others, was skeptical of the scramble for overnight riches. Yet as reports of huge profits began to accumulate, he too was bitten by the speculation bug. Together, the two Mizner brothers bought some 7,500 acres of land and formed the Mizner Development Corporation with the backing of some of Palm Beach's most respected names, including several Vanderbilts and General T. Coleman Du Pont. Grand and exclusive as Palm Beach was, Boca Raton was intended to put it in the shade. Elaborate plans were made for a Mediterranean paradise with twenty miles of canals bordered by homes costing $20,000 and up (this at a time when the average home sold for about $4,000). A large hotel, a small inn, and golf courses were to provide the focus for the development, while its showpiece was to be a million-dollar island palace for the architect himself. Harry Reichenbach, the greatest flim-flam man since P. T. Barnum, was hired to convince America that Boca Raton was to be the home of no one but blue-book celebrities and "you." The company's methods were ingenious and often lapsed into the outrageous and devious. To enhance the romantic past of the resort, for example, they invented tales of treasure having been buried there by pirates. Wilson Mizner turned his talents to the venture by burying a few doubloons and other relics and then arranging to have them discovered. The public took the bait.

Creating a lush and exotic garden environment was part of Addison Mizner's original plan for Boca Raton.

The sale of lots made the Mizners temporary millionaires. As fast as the money rolled in, Addison Mizner would divert it to making his architectural dreams a reality.

As an entrance to the development, the company built El Camino Real, a highway twenty lanes wide with a central canal sporting "Rialtos" and electrically driven Venetian gondolas. The road was less than half a mile long, but it caught the public's imagination nonetheless.

Addison also began work on the Cloister Inn—since enlarged and renamed the Boca Raton Hotel—and its attendant recreational facilities. The original parts of the structure still bear the marks of the master's hand. Mizner continued to work in the romantic Spanish Renaissance idiom he had established in his domestic designs at Palm Beach. Walls of pinkish-white stucco were topped by red tile roofs. The carved stone, wood, and enameled tile details were worked out with great care and finesse. Mizner hated buildings that looked too new or too consistent. Rather, he wanted his works to give the impression that they had evolved over the centuries—thus giving them an instant history—and he went to great lengths to modify and "age" his buildings as they were constructed. An asymmetrical floor plan, the juxtaposition of pointed and round-arched windows, the use of a Renaissance tower or loggia next to a Moorish courtyard or a Venetian water stair, and other devices all were employed to enhance the impression that the building was produced by a number of different craftsmen at various points in time, and to give it an organic feeling. Impromptu touches, such as an arched doorway leading to the back of a chimney or a staircase leading nowhere, were added solely for visual effect. New roofs were often deliberately broken and patched. Walls were smoked, smudged, and sprayed to simulate the effects of time.

Mizner used the same techniques on the interiors of the Cloister Inn. Many of the furnishings were Spanish and South American antiques picked up by the architect on his yearly plunder raids. Others were reproductions made in his own furniture factory, which were scratched, scarred, and stained into instant venerability in a matter of hours. Furniture, heraldic banners, vaulted wooden ceilings, and massive fireplaces all contributed to the atmosphere of Old World age and elegance.

Despite the very real architectural quality of Mizner's efforts, the Boca Raton development was doomed to failure. Investors were already nervous about how long the good times could last when General Du Pont, angered and alarmed by the Mizners'

Aerial view of the Cloister Inn shows its Venetian-like waterside view.
Inset: View into one of the courtyards

promotional distortions, denounced them as frauds. It was the beginning of the end. The Mizners tried to appear confident at the opening of the Cloister Inn in February 1926, but they were soon submerged in a wave of lawsuits. Addison's career, though far from ruined, was greatly affected. He died insolvent in 1933. Wilson Mizner was wiped out completely; he spent his last years in Hollywood as a screen writer for Warner Brothers.

With the collapse of the Florida land boom, the Cloister Inn's creditors stepped in to try to keep the enterprise afloat. Clarence H. Geist purchased the building and surrounding facilities in 1928 and set about bringing Mizner's dream to fruition. He acquired some 2,000 acres of what was now cheap land around the hotel and began a program of enlargement and revitalization. Schultze and Weaver of New York, the architects of the Breakers in Palm Beach, were commissioned to add 300 guest rooms and numerous public areas to the building. In 1930, the former Cloister Inn reopened as the Boca Raton Club. Members were required to invest $5,000 in the development of the area. Geist himself acted as a one-man screening committee and ruled the operations of the club like a tyrant. No event was allowed to begin until he was present. Despite terrible national economic conditions, the Boca Raton Club flourished through the 1930s.

Geist's architectural contributions to the hotel were extensive. Mizner's dining room became a lounge. Gold-leafed columns with richly carved stone capitals supported an arcade of pointed arches in the new "Cathedral" dining room. Another terrace and a movie theater were also added.

Like many of its counterparts, the Boca Raton Club served as an army training facility during World War II. In 1944, J. Myer Schine purchased the hotel and prepared it to serve wealthy vacationers once again. Arthur Vining Davis acquired the hotel and club in 1956; they remain under the control of the Arvida Corporation. Extensive changes have been made to allow the Boca Raton Hotel and Club to serve as a convention center. A twenty-six-story tower is the most noticeable addition, and despite its disproportionately large scale, there has been some attempt to let the base of the tower complete an existing courtyard. Recently, homes and private apartments that use the hotel's social and recreational facilities have been built on its grounds. Albeit on a much reduced scale, Addison Mizner's dreams for Boca Raton are being fulfilled.

The lobby, a part of the original Cloister Inn

MIAMI BEACH

Florida, 1920s and 1930s

"I'm going to build a city here! A city like magic, like romantic places you read and dream about, but never see," said Carl G. Fisher, the thirty-five-year-old automobile headlight magnate who was once described by Will Rogers as the midwife of Miami Beach. While Fisher was not the first to show an entrepreneurial interest in Miami Beach—or Ocean Beach, as it was then known—he was the first man who had both the vision and the financial ability to transform a swampy sand bar into one of America's greatest tropical resorts. Miami Beach came of age after World War I, when a combination of peace, prosperity, the phenomenal rise in automobile travel, and Fisher's beguiling publicity campaigns took effect.

The earliest commerical venture on Miami Beach was a coconut plantation that ended in failure in 1894. Through a series of financial arrangements, the original Lum Plantation was taken over by John Collins, an energetic Quaker from New Jersey who had been one of the original investors. Collins, for whom the main street in Miami Beach is still named, thought the property ideal for truck farming—this time for avocados instead of coconuts. His children and his son-in-law, Thomas Pancoast, had other ideas. Collins and Pancoast formed the Miami Beach Improvement Company, which allowed the older man to continue farming and the younger man to develop the area's potential for recreation. The pair eventually required the financial backing of Carl Fisher. After 1915, when Miami Beach became an incorporated town, these three men were most responsible for the development of the area.

Fisher established the Alton Beach Realty Company to develop his newly acquired property. His primary objective was the judicious and profitable sale of land. Thus, his luxury resort hotels were both winter playgrounds for the rich and famous and inducements to future development. The architectural quality of his hotels was important in establishing the over-all character and atmosphere of the development. Fisher built his hotels on sites overlooking the inland waterways, as Flagler had a generation earlier. (The oceanfront was not yet considered prime real estate.) His opulent hotels did indeed attract the desired investors. America's merchant princes—Harvey Firestone, Julius Fleischmann, J.C. Penney, James Snowden, Albert Champion, and others—bought land along Collins Avenue. The

The New Yorker Hotel embodies the streamlined image of Miami in the 1930s. All traces of historical association with the site have been removed.

The Nautilus Hotel at Miami Beach. Its island marina serviced guests' yachts.

houses these men built constituted the three-mile-long Millionaires Row that existed until the 1950s, when Miami Beach's second boom replaced the houses with new hotels.

The Flamingo Hotel was Fisher's first venture into the world of luxury resorts. Opening on New Year's Eve of 1920, the million-dollar hotel offered 150 rooms, lavishly decorated public spaces, and a well-manicured tropical landscape that contained numerous varieties of nonindigenous plants. The seemingly endless round of activities to amuse the guests included speedboating, polo matches, sunbathing, and dancing in the garden at teatime. The Flamingo was such a success that Fisher followed it with other luxury hotels: the Nautilus, the Boulevard, the Floridian, and the King Cole. To give the King Cole some additional class, he spent $50,000 to bring a group of polo stars from England to give demonstration matches and attract polo-playing American millionaires. As a further romantic embellishment to the conception of a British-style tropical paradise, the King Cole featured a buffet breakfast of kippers and kidneys. Guests invariably wore riding clothes and boots to breakfast, in direct emulation of the stars of the silent movies and of the polo players.

Other entrepreneurs followed Fisher's lead. Thomas Pancoast built the Pancoast Hotel, and N. B. T. Roney constructed the Roney Hotel. Interestingly, these two hotels were located on the oceanfront of Miami Beach and were the precursors of the development of ocean property in the late 1930s and 1950s.

All of these hotels were designed in a Mediterranean style that seemed natural in the Florida sunshine—a style which remains that state's strongest architectural tradition. The models for this Florida style were generally Italian villas and palazzi and Spanish baroque churches and palaces. By contrast, the concurrent Mediterranean Style in Southern California relied for models upon the simple, chaste farm buildings of southern Spain. The architectural elements of the Florida style included red tile roofs, pink- or beige-tinted stucco, wrought ironwork, and elaborate tilework. Open loggias, terraces, and courtyards not only accommodated pleasant outdoor living but seemed to affirm, in architectural terms, that Miami Beach was indeed a tropical paradise—an American Garden of Eden.

Fisher's earlier investments were now paying off. The mid-1920s found Miami Beach in the middle of an unprecedented boom; the euphoria and optimism seemed boundless. Here the denizens of the Jazz Age could come and play with abandon, gamble, dance, and drink bootleg liquor.

One of the most notorious establishments of this era was the Deauville Casino, built in 1924 by Joe Elsner, who sold real estate

from the back of his Rolls-Royce. In the 600-foot-long building located on the oceanfront, Elsner installed the "biggest pool, biggest dining room, and biggest gambling hall in Miami Beach." The University of Miami's symphony orchestra played Sunday nights on a platform suspended over the swimming pool. When the real estate boom burst because of the destructive hurricane of September 1926, Elsner lost the Deauville to creditors. By 1936, the building had been leased by new owner Lucy Cotton Thomas McGraw to Bernarr MacFadden, a physical culturist, food faddist, and publisher of True Confessions magazine. Known thereafter as the MacFadden-Deauville Hotel and Pleasure Resort, the old casino was transformed into a health spa that featured the "latest scientific discoveries of physiotherapy, hydrotherapy, and electrotherapy." While the facilities for regaining one's health were extensive, the promotional brochure noted that the spa did not accept as patrons "those who are bedridden or who are unable to care for themselves, those afflicted with tuberculosis, cancer, venereal disease, mental abnormalities, or contagious diseases of any kind." Obviously, one had to be pretty healthy to be admitted in the first place.

The Crash of 1929, following so closely the disastrious hurricane of 1926, put an end to development in Miami Beach—for a time, at least. With the loss of the massive financial investments and large crowds of the 1920s, Miami Beach could no longer sustain its glittering image, although the very rich continued to dance in the Flamingo's Oriental Tea Garden and to play polo at the King Cole. By 1940, the Beach was again experiencing good times. There was new development in the form of modest hotels at reasonable rates in the "South Beach" area. These hotels were not built in the lavish Mediterranean Style of the 1920s but in the new style of the late 1930s: Streamlined Moderne. Hotels such as the New Yorker, designed by Henry Hohauser in 1940, possessed simple but elegant modernistic features—curved corners, strip windows, vivid pastel colors, and ornamental horizontal and vertical stripes. It was during this period that Miami Beach came to resemble a kind of sun-drenched, tropical "City of the Future."

With the start of World War II, the new building boom came to a halt, and the resort facilities of the Beach were occupied by the Army Air Corps. Typically, the largest hotels of the 1920s were converted to hospitals. As late as 1945, one could still see the beach and the ocean from Collins Avenue. That view would vanish in the 1950s as Miami Beach experienced a second period of boom and decline.

The Pancoast Hotel at Miami Beach (inset) and the Miami Beach Biltmore at Coral Gables are but two examples of overgrown Mediterranean palazzi at Miami Beach.

HOTEL ROLYAT
Saint Petersburg, Florida

The Hotel Rolyat—that's Taylor spelled backwards—was constructed for owner Jack Taylor in Saint Petersburg in the waning days of the Florida land boom. The building was designed by a young Miami architect named Paul Reed and elaborately decorated inside by the John Wanamaker Company. The hotel was an exceedingly accomplished example of romantic stage-set Spanish architecture, not as fanciful as the designs of Addison Mizner, but with a strong plan and a scenographic sense of massing and detail.

Like many hotels, the Rolyat went under financially during the real estate bust of 1927. Between 1932 and 1951, the building was inhabited by the Florida Military Academy, and in 1954, it was taken over by the Stetson University College of Law. The Rolyat has been cared for by sympathetic users, and its spendid architectural qualities are still intact.

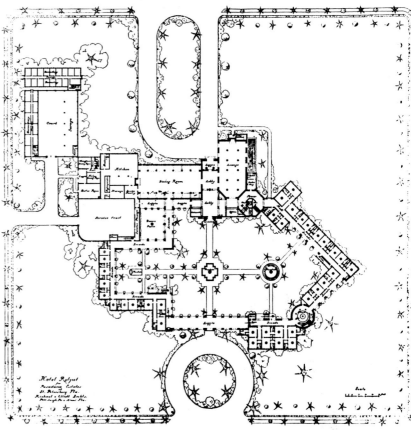

Above: Ground-floor plan. Left: Lobby at the Hotel Rolyat

SANTA BARBARA BILTMORE
Montecito, California

The Santa Barbara Biltmore is actually located in Montecito, a beautiful seaside community just to the east of Santa Barbara that has attracted the wealthy from across the country for the better part of a century. A list of local residents contains names like Armour, McCormick, Fleischmann, and Pillsbury. Fire destroyed Montecito's former premier hotel, the Potter, in 1921, and in 1926 realtor Harold S. Chase and billionaire C. K. G. Billings decided that a new hotel was needed. They acquired the oceanfront Walter Douglas estate for a hotel to be operated by the Bowman-Biltmore chain. The Santa Barbara Biltmore opened on December 12, 1926, with a gala attended by hotel operators from all along the California coast. In 1936 Allied Properties, Inc., bought the hotel, and in 1937 the Coral Casino Beach and Cabana Club opened adjacent to it. The Marriott chain now owns and operates it.

During the twenties, Santa Barbara was a beautiful town with an amazingly lush landscape and an awakening fondness for its Spanish past, with whose romance and exoticism the beauties of the place seemed to resonate. Several extremely successful buildings in the Spanish style soon won enthusiastic support from the Community Arts Association, and this lent considerable weight to the attempt to reinforce Santa Barbara's Spanish heritage. The townspeople fell in love with the look of white stucco walls and red tile roofs. When the town was severely damaged by an earthquake in 1925, the citizenry decided to rebuild the whole town in the Spanish mode.

Reginald Johnson, the architect chosen to design the Santa Barbara Biltmore, was one of the leading practitioners of the Spanish Colonial Revival Style in Southern California. He had already designed a number of large houses nearby. Johnson's feeling for domestic scale is apparent in the Santa Barbara Biltmore; the hotel building is entirely compatible with its residential surroundings. A low, rambling complex whose appearance belies its true size, it is an extremely picturesque composition of white walls and red tile roofs of various heights, suggesting the image of a small village. The guest rooms are placed in the wings, in turn arranged to form intimate garden courtyards. Cottages to the rear of the hotel proper give it an even more intimate and domestic ambience. Arched passageways and large

This hotel is like a romantic hacienda facing the Pacific Ocean, with the Santa Ynez Mountains looming up behind.

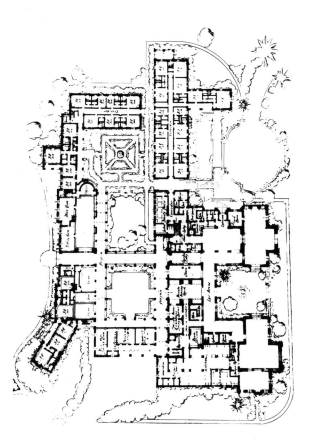

windows afford through-views that link the spaces visually and prevent any feeling of compartmentalization. Even relatively long spaces like the lobby and lounge are visually relieved by changes in level. The over-all atmosphere is one of intimacy and comfort.

Rich materials and elegant details also contribute to the building's charm. Balconies and wrought-iron railings decked with flower pots grace its windows. Inside, the floor is covered with terra-cotta tiles the color of seasoned leather, and the walls of the corridors are ornamented with a patterned tile dado. Several tile pictures illustrate scenes of local history. The philosophy of the management in decorating the hotel has been to change with the times while maintaining the original atmosphere. Some of the original furnishings are still in use, and new pieces are sympathetically Spanish in style. Only minor changes to the building have been necessary: a bar was added in the 1930s; the single large lounge was divided into three smaller ones; and the fountain was removed from the front courtyard to allow it to serve as an outdoor dining room. The spaces originally occupied by shops now serve private parties and convention groups. The Ship Room sports wood paneling, an arched ceiling, and porthole windows. This small private meeting room is hidden away up an unpretentious flight of spiral steps.

Because the Santa Barbara Biltmore was built in the wake of an earthquake, durable construction was of primary concern. The exposed beams in the lounge and dining room are made of reinforced concrete treated to look like wood. The deception is remarkably successful, and it points up Johnson's approach to the use of historical styles, which in turn was typical of his contemporaries. In an article in The Architect and Engineer in April 1929, Elmer Grey, architect of the Beverly Hills Hotel, described Johnson's use of Spanish forms:

Purity of style comes not from strict adherence to precedent, but from a sensitive feeling for the harmonies that constitute good style.... [Mr. Johnson] is not therefore a purist in style so far as strict adherence to precedent is concerned, but of that fine feeling which is more essential than anything else in the making of a pure style he is distinctly possessed.

The Santa Barbara Biltmore is obviously a modern building. Yet in its scale, massing, and details it alludes to an earlier time, remembered romantically as one of graciousness and ease.

Above: Ground-floor plan. The guest rooms and public spaces
are organized around lushly landscaped, sun-filled outdoor courtyards,
resulting in an efficiently organized building that is also full of charm.
Left, above: The hotel entrance
Left, below: The dining room with its concrete beam ceilings

BEVERLY HILLS HOTEL

Beverly Hills, California

The Beverly Hills Hotel was built in 1912 as the showplace of the development of the former Rodeo de las Aguas ranch. It was designed by Elmer Grey, one of the leading practitioners of the California Mission Revival Style. Although the hotel set the architectural standards for the community, today it is barely visible behind a wall of dense foliage along busy Sunset Boulevard.

The hotel has always been an exclusive home away from home for its well-heeled and famous guests. Stepping into its immaculately kept, comfortably furnished lobby is like walking back into the years of the 1930s and 1940s, when the Beverly Hills Hotel was host to the Hollywood movie colony. Indeed, one can still enjoy the thrill of catching a close-up glimpse of a star or two in the famous, if understated, Polo Lounge, whose hushed atmosphere is disrupted only by the loudspeaker used to call guests to the telephone. Famous names also blare out across the pool and are still audible several blocks away, indicating, it would seem, the desire of the stars and moguls to be anonymous but not forgotten. Forgotten they are not—at least not by the Beverly Hills Hotel. Careful records are made of each guest's preferences in food, drink, colors, and flowers to help them feel at home.

The red tile roofs, stucco walls, and towers of this hotel were intended to recall the early California missions.

MISSION INN

Riverside, California

The Mission Inn, originally known as the Glenwood Mission Inn, is one of the most astonishing architectural feasts in Southern California. For richness and profusion of form, color, and detail and for breath-taking spaces, the building has no peer in the region, except perhaps the Hotel Del Coronado and the Santa Barbara County Courthouse. Built in a style meant to evoke the "romance, traditions, and friendly spirit of early California," the hotel features both an episodic, stage-set Spanish ambience and an array of facilities intended to enhance the effects of sun, landscape, and the mountain view. The Mission Inn took shape over the years because of the sustained vision of its proprietor, Frank Miller, who clearly saw that the legends and myths of Southern California could be combined with contemporary planning and construction to produce a place full of arcadian delights.

Glenwood Cottage, the predecessor of the Mission Inn, was opened as a hotel in 1876 by C. C. Miller, the father of Frank Miller. Located in Riverside, in one of the many pleasant inland valleys of Southern California devoted to agriculture, the cottage was important as a stopping place. With the coming of the railroad in the 1880s, it accommodated both tourists enjoying their first taste of an American Mediterranean climate and settlers seeking to establish new roots in the region of orange and avocado groves.

In 1902, Arthur B. Benton, a Los Angeles architect, designed a substantial addition to the original adobe building. Benton was a consulting architect for the Landmarks Club, founded early in 1896 by California author and regional promoter Charles Fletcher Lummis to encourage the restoration of the fast-disintegrating Southern California missions. Thus he was an authority on mission architecture, and his designs for the Glenwood Mission Inn were influential in establishing Mission Revival as the architectural style for a number of other major buildings in Riverside, including a Carnegie library.

The new addition was loosely patterned after the Hotel Colorado in Glenwood Springs, which Miller had seen on a trip to the East that also included visits to the Hotel Alvarado in Albuquerque, New Mexico, and the Mohonk and Minnewaska Mountain Houses in New York. In Benton's design, the main building ran east-

A view from the ornate doorway of the hotel's Saint Francis Chapel shows a courtyard and guest rooms beyond.

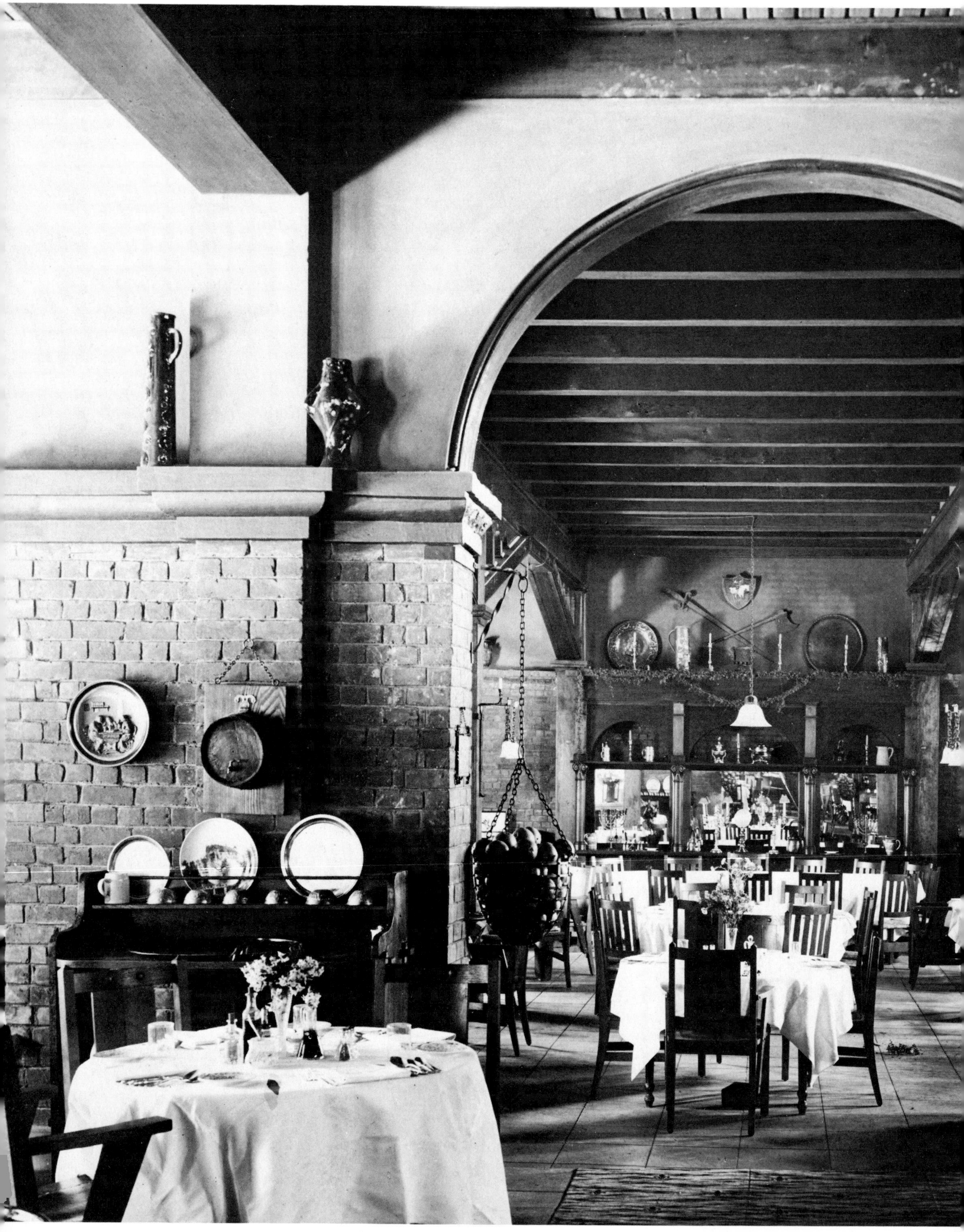

west; two perpendicular wings projected southward to create a large courtyard with a southern exposure, surrounded by a grape-arbored pergola and filled with palms, pepper trees, and a profusion of tropical plants. On the top level of the four-story building, the 700-foot Paseo de las Palmas provided a place to bask or stroll in the sun and view the ring of high mountains to the north and east, or Mount Rubidoux, jutting up out of the valley floor to the west. Adding interest to this rooftop garden were dormers and the first of Frank Miller's collection of rare mission and cathedral bells brought from Baja California and South America.

Public spaces were furnished with Mission Style furniture designed by Gustav Stickley and William Morris, and with Oriental rugs. Dark-stained woodwork and natural brick complemented the light-colored plaster walls. Great attention was paid to details. For example, iron latches were used throughout instead of door-knobs. The doors themselves were of broad stained boards, each incised with the design of the Indian river of life. The total effect was one of subdued and tasteful luxury. The new hotel may have reflected the interest in the California missions in its imagery and furnishings, but it was thoroughly modern in its planning and construction. Fireproof throughout, the walls were constructed of concrete and cement tile covered with rough plaster to resemble adobe. Every room had a bathroom, a long-distance telephone, and steam heat—all very advanced for that day. Sixty-five rooms had picturesque lava-brick fireplaces.

The first guests in the expanded hotel were, predictably and appropriately, a Raymond and Whitcomb party of 48 tourists from Boston, who arrived on January 22, 1903. They found a hotel whose style of architecture, furniture, and finishing hardware all conspired to reinforce, indeed literally to create, an image of early California days—an image as patently contrived as it was beguiling. The national importance of the hotel was established in 1907 when President Theodore Roosevelt stayed overnight and was guest of honor at a lavish banquet. Before departing, Roosevelt dutifully officiated at the transplanting of the first navel orange tree to the main courtyard.

In 1909, Miller began a second major addition to the hotel. The exterior of Benton's new Cloister Wing was heavily influenced by the San Gabriel Mission and featured a tower closely patterned after that of the mission at Carmel. The new Spanish baronial music room, with a cathedral pipe organ built by the Kimball Company of Chicago, could seat 500 people. Fifty guest rooms were added, as was an interior cloistered walk where statues and

The high, beamed dining room is furnished with dark Mission Style furniture.

206

Above: President Roosevelt transplanting a navel orange tree. Below: The entrance courtyard as seen early in this century

Above: A few of Frank Miller's collection of bells on display. Below: The hotel looms up around the Garden of the Bells.

paintings depicting the era of the Franciscan padres were displayed. The Garden of the Bells provided a home for Miller's growing bell collection. The roof level of the new addition was devoted to sport, including tennis and roller skating. There was an observatory in the Carmel Tower. Other pavilions in the highly sculptural roofscape housed accommodations for music and craft studios and several uniquely decorated penthouse suites.

In 1911, Frank Miller traveled to Europe, collecting numerous paintings and artifacts in Spain. These were displayed in the Art Gallery and in the Spanish Patio, both designed by Myron Hunt in 1914. The Spanish Patio to this day is filled with the scent of blossoming orange trees. The main kitchen, also designed by Hunt and named for a patron saint—La Cocina de San Pasqual—continued the general Spanish theme of the hotel. Yellow and blue tiles, interspersed with heraldic arms, covered the walls, and red tiles covered the floor. Unlike most hotel kitchens, this one was designed to be an important and visible part of the atmosphere of the place, and guests were invited in to see it.

Construction continued over the years: the Oriental Court of 1925, the Rotunda International of 1929, and the Saint Francis Chapel of 1932, all designed by Stanley Wilson. The Rotunda, a tall round courtyard lined with open stairways spiraling from the ground-level entrance up to the roofscape, recalls great skylighted interior commercial spaces such as the Bradbury Building in Los Angeles. In 1948, after Miller's death, the remaining portions of the original adobe house were destroyed to permit construction of a swimming pool.

The rapid urbanization of Southern California in the years after World War II disastrously altered the special combination of clean air, lush orange groves, and arcadian atmosphere that had made Riverside a successful resort town. Without Miller's strong personality and vision to guide the hotel, it began an irreversible slide into chronic financial difficulties. Many of its collections and furnishings were sold, and there was frequent talk of demolition. Fortunately, it was rescued in the 1970s by a foundation composed of citizens of Riverside, and is currently undergoing restoration and partial conversion to apartments and commercial space.

The legendary qualities of both Frank Miller and his Mission Inn were extolled in a tribute by David Starr Jordan, then president of Stanford University:

It has been left to you, Frank Miller, a genuine Californian, to dream of the hotel that ought to be, to turn your dream into plaster and stone, and to give us in mountain-belted Riverside the one hotel which a Californian can recognize as his own.

The Rotunda International: hotel shops around an open atrium and spiral staircase

The Spanish baronial Music Room, where daily concerts were performed

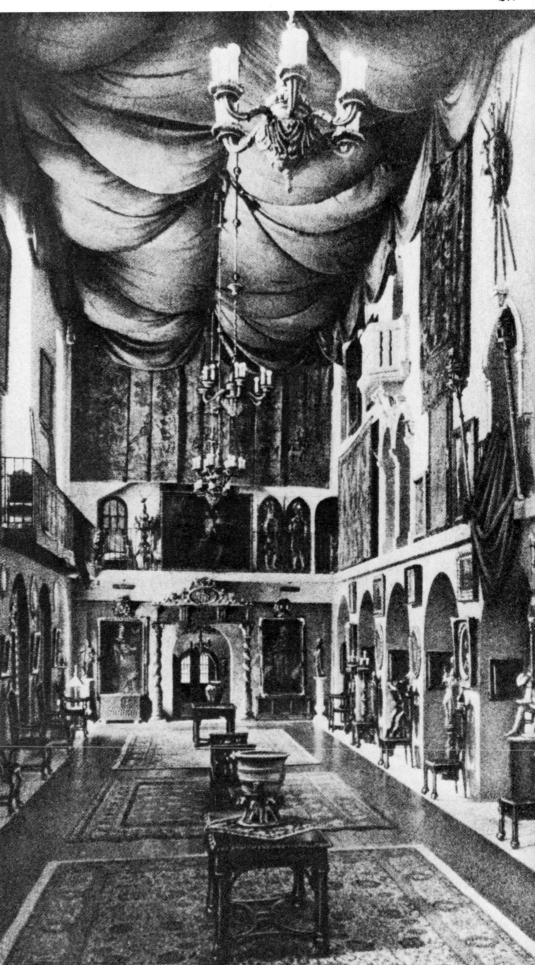

An interior cloister walk with paintings, sculpture, and a tented ceiling

LA FONDA HOTEL

Santa Fe, New Mexico

La Fonda Hotel was built by the Santa Fe Railway and managed by Fred Harvey. By the early 1920s, when the hotel was built, the picturesque Spanish-Indian style had become extremely popular in New Mexico. Like many of the historic structures of Santa Fe, La Fonda is organized around an interior courtyard. But instead of the traditional adobe walls, architects Rapp, Rapp and Henrickson employed reinforced concrete and structural tile covered with rough cement stucco. Terraces, wooden balconies, projecting "vegas," and rustic interiors were artfully contrived to achieve a very traditional appearance in what is actually a very modern structure.

The building fuses picturesque elements redolent of Indian pueblos with the features of a modern hotel.

ARIZONA BILTMORE

Phoenix, Arizona

The Arizona Biltmore exhibits a very different response to its site than do other hotels of the 1920s. The Biltmore's architects sought to capture the character of the desert in the materials and massing of the building. They did not adopt a romantic style that alluded to the history and climate of the site, but neither did they employ a style stripped of all decoration for purposes of economy.

Charles and Warren McArthur promoted the Biltmore project and their younger brother, Albert, designed the building. Albert had been one of the draftsmen trained in Frank Lloyd Wright's Oak Park studio twenty years earlier. Convinced of the practicality and economy of using concrete block as a building material in the desert, he asked his old teacher, who had developed an unusual reinforced-concrete-block construction system in California several years before, to come to Phoenix to help in applying it to the hotel. Wright, who had few commissions of his own at the time, gladly joined the effort as a behind-the-scenes consultant. The powerful impress of his ideas is apparent in all aspects of the design. Wright was greatly moved and excited by the rugged grandeur of the desert:

Arizona character seems to cry out for a space-loving architecture of its own. The straight line and flat plane must come here — of all places — but they should become the dotted line, the broad low extended plane textured, because in all this astounding desert there is not one hard undotted line to be seen. The great masonry we see rising from the great mesa floors is... not architecture at all, but it is inspiration. A pattern of what appropriate Arizona architecture might well be lies there hidden in the sahuaro, a perfect example of reinforced building construction.

The two architects shared a desire to harmonize the forms, lines, patterns, and colors of their building with those of the desert. Despite these common goals, the experience was frustrating for both men. McArthur was in the difficult position of trying to exercise authority over his former teacher. Wright, accustomed to maintaining strong control over a design, was frustrated when his ideas were modified. The addition of a fourth floor, for example, robbed the building of its strong hori-

A grouping of specially made furniture around a fireplace made of the patterned concrete blocks used throughout the building

Left: The lobby of the Arizona Biltmore. Above: The traditionally uniformed doorman

zontal appearance, and improper application of Wright's modular block construction system eliminated many of its expected economies.

Nevertheless, the Arizona Biltmore was an architectural success. The concrete blocks were molded and cured right on the site, and many of them were sculptured with abstract geometrical patterns inspired by desert plant forms. The use of concrete block as a dominant element, exposed inside and out, set up a consistent construction module that related the dimensions of all the parts of the building and produced a great sense of calm and visual unity in the hotel. The warm grey color of the concrete walls acted as a foil for bright fabrics and for the furniture, designed by the architects and fabricated by W. and J. Sloane. Leaving the walls unpainted also meant that only the floors and ceilings needed to be considered for decorative treatment. A dull green stain was used to enliven the concrete floors, while parts of the ceiling were covered in gold leaf. Wright was fond of pointing out that the latter was actually economical in that gold leaf required little maintenance.

The lighting was integrated into the concrete block system. White milk-glass light blocks were set into the structural piers and into the corbels supporting the beams in the lobby. The roof and the trim throughout the building were of sheet copper, chemically treated to give it a soft blue-green color.

The floor plan too had its share of unusual features. One visiting hotel man wrote:

The lobby is over two hundred and fifty feet in length, but so arranged with ... registration desk, great stairways ... modernistic wrought iron gates at the entrance to the sun room, wide easy steps to the dining room, short hallways to numerous verandas, and pleasing halls to the shops and broker's office, that its immense size is lost in review of its graceful proportions.

The other spaces that excited the comment of guests and the architectural press were the octagonal ballroom with its "flying rafters with copper facings that lend a cobwebby appearance" and the dining room "of noble proportions" with its "expansive golden ceiling" and murals by Maynard Dixon. The guest rooms were large and simply but elegantly furnished. To the Squaw Peak side of the

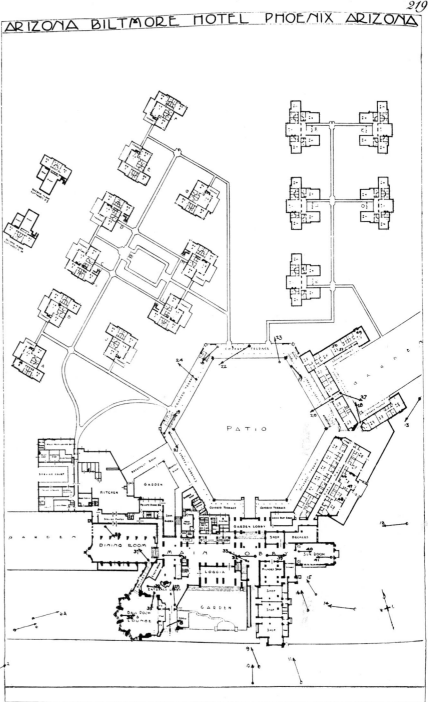

ARIZONA BILTMORE HOTEL PHOENIX ARIZONA

Above: The plan shows the main building and the outlying cottages. Left: The swimming pool

hotel lay a number of private cottages with "velvety green" lawn in front of them; "the all-embracing view from their roof porches and generous verandas covers limitless plain, rugged mountain and sinuous stretches of the great canal." A golf course and riding trails were laid out among the sahuaro cactus. In keeping with the image of an oasis in the desert, extensive gardens were developed around the hotel with trees, shrubs, and flowers imported from all over the world to provide green freshness and seasonal color. Beyond the limits of the gardens lay the majestic desert, the newest form of the rediscovered American wilderness, and at a distance rose Camelback Mountain, the setting sun tinting its peak with wonderful pastel colors and deep shadows.

THE AHWAHNEE
Yosemite National Park, California

By 1880, the magnificent Yosemite Valley was one of California's primary attractions. Tourists endured the expense and discomfort of long, dusty stagecoach journeys —largely, it seems, because they felt obliged to. The marvels of the place were for the most part lost on them as they surveyed its celebrated features by carriage from the valley floor. John Muir scorned the apathy of fashionable ladies in the face of nature:

They climb sprawlingly to their saddles like overgrown frogs pulling themselves up a streambank through the bent sedges, ride up the valley with about as much emotion as the horses they ride upon and, comfortable when they have "done it all," long for the safety and flatness of their proper homes.

Muir rejoiced that few tourists felt compelled to see more than the prescribed views, but were content to spend their time "floating slowly about the bottom of the valley as a harmless scum, collecting in hotel and saloon eddies, leaving the rocks and falls eloquent as ever and instinct with imperishable beauty and greatness."

By the 1920s, the growing interest in outdoor life, the provision of inexpensive camp facilities, and improved roads had made the attractions of the Yosemite much more democratic. Yet park managers realized that the opening of an all-year highway in 1926 would call for a new year-round lodging facility, one that would offer the luxurious accommodations that wealthy and refined tourists had long been demanding. Consequently, the park's chief concessionaire, the Yosemite Park and Curry Company, began planning a new hotel in 1925. A site long occupied by stables was chosen for its excellent views of Yellowstone Falls, Half Dome, and Glacier Point. One of the company's directors, Harry Chandler, the powerful editor of the Los Angeles Times, suggested that Gilbert Stanley Underwood be retained as architect.

Underwood was only thirty-five-years-old at the time, but he had already made a name for himself as the designer of several large stations for the Union Pacific Railroad. His undeniable flair for the dramatic made him well suited to the job, and he quickly produced a scheme for a grand three-winged, six-story, steel-framed structure faced with rough granite boulders and concrete patterned and stained

The architect, Gilbert Stanley Underwood (far right), and his clients hold a rendered elevation drawing of the Ahwahnee.

to resemble redwood. The appearance of the hotel was just as the directors had hoped it would be, but its functional planning was awkward indeed. After the first of many battles with the willful Underwood over proposed changes, the design was approved and the contract let to a San Francisco contractor for $525,000.

Work began immediately. The price of the building rose steadily as architect, manager, and contractor argued over changes, and the final cost was almost double the initial estimate. The job of decorating and furnishing the interiors was given to nationally known art historians Phyllis Ackerman and Arthur Pope and interior designer Dorothy Simpson, who later became art director for the hotel. The fabrics, rugs, murals, and accessories used geometric patterns drawn from Southwestern Indian blankets and baskets. The results bear a resemblance to contemporary Art Deco designs. Other elements of the interior decoration reflect the influence of Bavaria, Tudor England, Persia, and the early days of California: the designers had cosmopolitan tastes. To their credit, everything from the German Gothic chandeliers to the hand-loomed Indian bedspreads seems appropriate to the hotel.

As the opening date for the hotel approached, it was named the "Ahwahnee," meaning, in the local Indian dialect, "deep grassy valley." Last-minute problems with unexpected automobile noise necessitated construction of a new entry. The painters barely finished in time to avoid bumping into the first guests. The building opened in June 1927.

The Ahwahnee was snobbish and off-limits to the general coatless-and-tieless public, to the irritation of many who regarded the Yosemite as a bastion of democratic pleasures. Even some of the guests were annoyed. Herbert Hoover, then secretary of commerce, almost checked out in disgust when a disdainful doorman refused to admit him in his rumpled fishing clothes. Gradually the expense of operation and the financial pinch of the Depression caused the hotel to relax many of its rules and restrictions, lower its rates, and accept a more informal ambience.

With the exception of three years of rough treatment as a naval hospital during World War II, the Ahwahnee has been open continuously and played host to some six million visitors. Vacations there are a tradition for many families. Those who make a point of attending the hotel's annual re-enactment of Washington Irving's Sketch Book account of Christmas dinner at Bracebridge Hall must make their reservations nearly a year in advance.

The Ahwahnee is well ensconced in the rugged landscape of Yosemite National Park.

Top: The rustic exterior of rough stone and wood is only a beguiling skin over a modern steel structure, shown during construction.
Above and left: Inside, the rooms are spacious, suave, and sophisticated stage sets of elegant vacations.

TIMBERLINE LODGE

Mount Hood, Oregon

The Timberline Lodge is one of the best examples of the regional mountain-resort architecture of the Northwest. During the 1930s, when skiing became a popular sport, it was decided that the Works Progress Administration would join with private managers to build much-needed hotel accommodations on the upper slopes of Mount Hood. Architect W. I. Turner and the personnel of the United States Forest Service Regional Engineer's Office designed the building with the advice of consultant Gilbert Stanley Underwood, already well known for his work at Yosemite and Sun Valley. The Oregon Art Project, a state public works group, was given responsibility for decorating and furnishing the interiors, thereby providing jobs for unemployed artists and craftsmen.

The lodge was carefully sited to take advantage of fabulous views of the Cascades and to avoid long-term damage to the delicate vegetation. The building represents a new idea of what a wilderness hotel should look like. The historical forms and rustic details prevalent in park hotels of previous decades are absent. Whereas earlier wilderness hotels resembled very large log cabins, the Timberline Lodge exhibits a more streamlined, compact, abstract form typical of the 1930s; its style could be called Deco Rustic. The lower portions of the building are massive rocklike forms that seem to be an outgrowth of the site. The large, simple, pyramidal roofs that extend almost to the ground in places echo the shapes of the mountains.

The internal organization is straightforward. Activities related to the comings and goings of day skiers are located on the ground floor. The main floor contains the multistory lounge, dining room, and kitchen. Guest rooms and dormitory accommodations are on the floors above.

The natural wood interiors present a harmonious background for the furniture and other decorative arts. Newel posts fashioned from old cedar telephone poles are carved with animal figures to recall totem poles. Wrought iron and rawhide adorn the massive wooden furniture. The wagon-wheel and ox-yoke lighting fixtures allude blatantly to the pioneer past, while paintings and murals depict historical events and wonders of the state.

The hand-crafted character of Timberline Lodge is reinforced by many details, such as these gates at the entrance to the dining room.

Part of Bedroom Suite - Timberline Lodge

Each guest room has a distinctive decoration and color scheme based on the watercolors of wild flowers that adorn its walls. The upholstery and bedspreads are of handwoven Oregon flax and wool and the draperies of hand-appliquéd cotton or linen. The original hooked rugs were made from scraps discarded by WPA sewing units and from old clothing and blankets donated by the Civilian Conservation Corps.

Above: A two-story lounge. Below: A typical room. Left: The hotel during winter and summer

ROYAL HAWAIIAN HOTEL

Waikiki Beach, Hawaii

The Royal Hawaiian Hotel, known as the "Pink Palace of the Pacific," sits on a 16-acre site long associated with Hawaiian royalty. King Kalanikapule built his seaside home here overlooking Waikiki Beach. The same site was later selected by King Kamehameha, upon the occasion of his conquest of the island of Oahu, for a summer home for his queen, Kaahumann.

Typically, the decision to build a first-class resort hotel at Waikiki was made by the company that brought the bulk of tourist traffic to the islands. The Matson Navigation Company was eager to add a luxury cruise ship to its fleet. In order to attract affluent travelers, there would have to be a luxurious hotel at the destination. As a result, major landowners Castle and Cook, together with the Territorial Hotel Company, built the 410-room Royal Hawaiian in 1925, at a cost of about $4,000,000.

The architect for the six-story pink stucco building was the firm of Warren and Wetmore of New York, designers of the Broadmoor Hotel and Grand Central Terminal. While the style has been attributed to the influence of the movies, particularly the Spanish-Moorish sets from Rudolph Valentino's film The Sheik, the hotel is a good if not unusual example of the romantic Spanish architecture so popular in the 1920s. Surely the most distinctive feature of the building is its pink color, the maintenance of which requires 1,300 gallons of paint per coat. One explanation for the choice of color is that it recalls the coral stone of Queen Kaahumann's summer palace. Another story has it that Charles Wetmore, the architect, was charmed by the pink house in which he stayed during all his visits to the site. Both tales are a bit far-fetched, but in any case the hotel lingers powerfully in one's memory because of the contrast between the vibrantly colored building, the lush green beauty of the grounds and gardens, and the brilliant blue of sky and sea.

On February 1, 1927, the hotel opened to the public with a party attended by 1,200 guests. The event properly marked the emergence of the Hawaiian Islands as the "Playground of the Pacific." The very rich now had a third American tropical paradise in which to roam, a luxury ocean liner on which to sail there, and a hotel at which to stay upon arrival. Boats from the Mainland docked at Pier 9. Arrival in

The hotel orchestra, its conductor, and the lead singer pose for a portrait in the 1930s, during the early heyday of the Royal Hawaiian Hotel.

Honolulu was marked by as many as 200 people from the various hotels, greeting new guests with fresh flower leis. Departures from the islands were equally dramatic: the beach boys who had dived for tossed coins upon arrival would now dive from the departing boat as it passed in front of the Royal Hawaiian and swim in to the hotel's beach.

The last years of the 1920s and the entire 1930s were a fabled time at the Royal Hawaiian. Movie stars arrived regularly from Hollywood, including Clark Gable, who spent one of his honeymoons here. Most people came to escape the Northern winters. Many of them brought their own servants and occasionally even their own silk sheets. Guests were capably served by a staff of 300. Mr. and Mrs. Henry J. Rogers, Jr., unnotable but typical guests, arrived for their honeymoon in the late 1920s, bringing with them their Hispano-Suiza convertible to tour the miles of scenic roads that ringed Oahu.

Although the Depression severely reduced the number of visitors from the Mainland, the Royal Hawaiian remained a favorite spot with celebrities such as the Rockefellers, Fords, and Roosevelts. Even in those hard times, the hotel possessed a world-wide reputation as a first-class resort. After serving as a rest-and-recreation center for the United States Navy during World War II, it reopened to the public on February 1, 1947. Today, the Royal Hawaiian is surrounded and to some extent dwarfed by tall hotels of a more recent vintage. Nevertheless, it remains an enclave of casually elegant ways in its oasis of lush landscaping. One's memory of the place still includes coconut, banyan, poinciana, papaya, and hibiscus trees, the beach with the view of Diamond Head beyond, and the soft sea breezes rustling through the potted palms on the covered porches.

The hotel and its lush gardens, with Waikiki Beach and the vast Pacific Ocean in the background

A typical International Style hotel in Miami Beach

Since World War 11

The Second World War severely curtailed the business of American resorts, already crippled by the ongoing effects of the Depression. Not that the somber events in Europe and the Pacific dampened vacationers enthusiasm; many people would gladly have taken the opportunity to get away from the daily routine for a brief time. But the nation's energies were totally focused on the war effort. Gasoline rationing limited travel, and the shortage of necessary manpower reduced hotel staffs to skeleton crews. The unavailability of building materials prevented all but the most necessary repairs. While many resorts were saved from financial ruin by conversion into military hospitals and training camps, the hotel buildings themselves often fared poorly. Crude, expedient remodeling and hard use by military tenants damaged many venerable buildings.

At the close of the war, most hotels were returned to civilian management and long-neglected repairs were made. Some, like the Broadmoor, began ambitious programs of expansion, adding new buildings and sports facilities while completely refurbishing and updating their existing physical plant. These efforts were well repaid, for, as after the First World War, the American people were anxious to forget the hard times and to enjoy themselves. Resort hotels experienced a new wave of prosperity.

In the postwar era, hotels were faced with some rough competition in the form of the motel. This new type of hostelry had first appeared during the 1920s, but its image was one of seediness, due in part to its roadside location. In addition to catering to a less affluent transient clientele, the motel was popularly maligned as a setting for illicit rendezvous. After World War II, however, auto tourists who wanted to stay only a few days in any one place, and who insisted on having facilities and points of interest convenient to the road, began to have a tremendous impact. Resort motels appeared along the roads of America, offering comfortable accommodation near scenic and historic attractions. Motels made a serious effort to upgrade both their facilities and their reputations, aided by the standards established by the new national chains. They now offered rooms and restaurants on a par with hotels and with the added conveniences of easy access and lower prices. In addition, the atmosphere of a motel was less formal, and the expense of tipping was eliminated. At first, hotel men dismissed the threat of competition; in their view, motels served a different class of customer. The appearance of the luxury motel and the motor hotel in the early 1950s blurred such distinctions. The motel, as a building type, has undergone an evolution too complex to discuss here, but we would like to draw attention to one in particular whose style and spirit have much in common with resort hotels of the turn of the century.

The Madonna Inn, by the side of the highway near San Luis Obispo, California, was built (and is still being built) as a labor of love by highway contractor Alex Madonna and his wife, Phyllis. The exterior style of the place is more or less storybook "Italian-Swiss Chalet," rendered in massive boulders and fanciful wooden scrollwork. This whimsical image sets the tone for the interior decoration of the public rooms and the 109 guest suites. The coffee shop is a symphony of carved spindle work, stained glass, hammered copper, and trompe-l'oeil wall murals. Past the lobby with its massive fireplace constructed of enormous boulders, some of which weigh as much as fifteen tons, is the dining room, dazzling with its mirrored walls, gilding, and plum upholstery. The adjacent bar is entered through wooden portals festooned with bunches of carved grapes. Downstairs, the grotto rest rooms attract a steady crowd of the curious who simply must see the sea-shell sinks and, in the men's room, the waterfall urinal. Each of the guest rooms follows a different theme, suggested by names like "Cloud Nine" and "Victorian Gardens."

Just as the automobile had altered the established railroad-resort patterns, the airplane greatly extended the travel range of the affluent vacationer and led to

the development of new resort areas and new patterns of travel. The desire to explore fresh scenery and the competitive urge to stay one step ahead of the masses inspired knowledgeable and experienced resorters to seek out new playgrounds. Florida and California became more accessible than ever before. The three-day train trip from Chicago to Los Angeles, for example, was reduced to hours by airplane. As in the nineteenth century, accessibility led quickly to mass travel. Once air routes were established, the airlines and hotel companies—which were sometimes one and the same—began vigorous promotion of the new spots to assure their popularity. Budget air fares and off-season bargain rates were developed to keep business brisk during less desirable times of the year. Places like Miami, with its good winter climate, experienced a tremendous boom in hotel construction that ended only in the late 1950s, as developers and airlines recognized the advantages offered by the combination of exotic settings and lower land, construction, and labor costs in Mexico and on the islands of the Caribbean. Hawaii, too, experienced a similar growth bonanza once air ties with the Mainland were established.

The typical high-rise slabs constructed everywhere during this period were economical to build and efficient to operate, though they usually lacked a strong affinity with their sites. Still, the governments of underdeveloped areas in the Caribbean, Latin America, and the South Pacific were quite willing to encourage the building of these hotels. As it had been in the nineteenth century in our own undeveloped Western states, the contemporary resort hotel was a symbol of the modern age and a stimulus to further investment.

Postwar architecture abided by the tenets of the International Style, or what is popularly thought of as "modern" architecture. This style took form in Europe in the 1920s when architects like Walter Gropius, Mies van der Rohe, and Le Corbusier sought to reject all ties with the architectural past and to create a new architecture appropriate to the modern era. These men glorified the technological miracles of the twentieth century and transformed them into acceptable aesthetic models. Emphasis was placed on the forthright use of glass, steel, and concrete and upon a simple appearance. Applied ornament was taboo. Instead, the proportions and detailing of the structural materials themselves were viewed aesthetically. In its pure form, the International Style required the elimination of all unessential visual elements. Buildings in this style therefore tended to look austere, particularly to the layman accustomed to the

The vast lobby of the Contemporary Hotel at Walt Disney World

Above: Disney World's Polynesian Hotel. Below: A ski village at Lake Tahoe

rich decorative interest of older structures. In addition, because one of the tenets of the International Style was the idea of the universal space wherein one architectural form can suit all purposes and all places, resort hotels in this style tended to resemble office buildings and apartment houses—precisely the symbols of the environment that the vacationer hoped to escape. Yet despite the inappropriateness of the International Style for resort buildings, architects who used decoration or forms associated with the past were regarded as reactionary. Architects and hotel men were faced with the difficult decision whether to follow the dictates of modern architecture or to address the demand for creating a dramatic and distinctive resort atmosphere. Through the 1950s and into the mid-1960s, however, most resort hotels were constructed in accordance with the principles of the International Style.

In an effort to give the pristine forms of modern architecture greater appeal, designers turned to abstract art for inspiration. Many of the hotels of the early 1950s used broad curving forms, superimposed abstract shapes, and bright colors to suggest a relaxed and festive mood. Often local crafts and decorative arts were employed to supplement the otherwise standard furnishings. Local materials were introduced sparingly to give recognizable atmosphere and a sense of place. In the Pacific Islands, for example, bamboo might cover a lounge ceiling, and a native mask might grace a lava-stone wall. But the over-all image remained clean, attractive—and a trifle dull.

Not all hotel owners were enthusiastic about modern architecture. Ben Novack insisted that Morris Lapidus design his new Miami Beach hotel, the Fontainebleau, in a traditional style to cater to the ostentatious proclivities of his patrons. The architect responded with a sensuously curved contemporary building that sported a free interpretation of French Renaissance decor on the interior, replete with antiques, gilt ornament, and crystal chandeliers. Other architects were aghast at the richness, the historicism, and the movie-set quality of it all, but the guests loved it. It offered them a glamorous, exciting, and ostentatious life quite unlike their everyday routine. The Fontainbleau became the model of the expensive luxury hotel of the late 1950s.

The insistent opulence of such a hotel did not appeal to everyone. In contrast, a number of resorts appeared that offered the harried urban dweller a chance to escape to a small-scaled world of peace, quiet, and informal relaxation. Some of the new hideaways were conversions of older structures of distinctive architectural character. The Habitation Le Clerc near Port-au-Prince, Haiti, was once the estate of Napoleon's sister. Laurance Rockefeller's Caneel Bay Plantation on Saint John in the Virgin Islands was designed to resemble a village with simple but carefully executed stone and wood guest cottages, recalling indigenous native dwellings set in a lush tropical landscape.

The second-home or condominium resort began to grow in popularity during the early 1960s. To complement the individual cottage or condominium unit, a lodge is often included to act as the recreational and social center and to provide accommodations and meeting facilities for visitors. Agreements permitting the management to rent the living unit during those parts of the year when the owner is elsewhere allow such a complex to operate much like a conventional resort hotel.

Even though glamorous ski resorts have existed since the 1930s in places like Sun Valley, Idaho, they have become a popular resort form only in the past two decades. Just after World War II, most developers thought that ski areas were attractive primarily for day outings, and they aimed their promotions largely toward regional clientele. The architectural style of these earlier ski resorts usually reflected the small-scale vernacular buildings of the region. By the late 1950s, skiing had developed an international appeal, and European resorts became the models for American developments. Chalets brought an Alpine air to American ski resorts. By the late 1960s, some modern high-rise hotels and condominiums had been built for the sake of efficiency, economy, and higher-density use. Yet for the most part, the preferred scale has remained small and domestic, often taking the form of simple shed-roofed structures reminiscent of farm or mining buildings familiar in many regions.

Resorts of the village type embody a much more direct and dependent relationship between the architecture and the character of the site than do large hotels at places like Miami Beach and Las Vegas. The Club Med chain of resorts, for example, emphasizes site development and outdoor activities to such an extent that the resort hotel building itself is all but eliminated. Places like this approach an image of the Garden of Eden itself, an innocent playground where formality plays no part. Everyday settings, clothing, and roles and every taint of commercialism are swept away. A well-organized, low-key social schedule keeps vacationers happily and almost constantly employed—as though boredom were the only forbidden fruit in paradise.

In contrast to the resort that relies almost exclusively on the attributes of its site is the resort that is almost totally isolated from its surroundings. Apart from the advantages of a good climate, the desert landscape around Las Vegas and the oceanfront setting of Miami Beach rarely enter into the visitor's experience. The perpetually nocturnal world of the casino and the poolside oasis are far more engaging and comfortable places to be. These self-contained resorts are direct descendants of those nineteenth-century Western hotels where resorters seldom strayed from the clipped gardens and the shady porches.

Where the site is considered relatively unimportant, the burden of creating a memorable and enjoyable atmosphere falls heavily upon the architecture. Through the manipulation of imagery, scale, materials, and color, a building can allude to any place and time, real or make-believe, that will catch the guests' fancy. This thematic approach to design is used in Las Vegas, resulting in a wide array of fantastic images ranging from Roman decadence to Hollywood nostalgia. The thematic hotels of Walt Disney World exemplify a more carefully coordinated effort to create a large-scale fantasy setting. Apparently disturbed by the uncontrolled growth surrounding Disneyland in Anaheim, California, Disney acquired 2,500 acres of swampland near Orlando, Florida, at a relatively low cost, enabling Disney Enterprises to reshape the very landscape and control every aspect of the development. They could now protect the atmosphere that they were creating so carefully. Ultimately, there will be five hotels at Disney World, each embodying a distinctive theme. The Contemporary and Polynesian hotels are already in operation. Ironically, both of them are constructed of the same prefabricated one-room modules, manufactured by United States Steel Corporation; only the applied thematic decoration is different. In the next few years. Asian, Persian, and Venetian hotels will be built of the same modular units elsewhere along the shore of Disney World's man-made lake and linked by both water and monorail transportation to the main park itself. This development is probably the best example of a totally man-made, self-contained tourist attraction.

There is little reason to believe that resort hotels will be startlingly different in the future. They will continue to respond to the changing life-styles and interests of their patrons. We noticed with pleasure the recent appearance of a resort in the West which caters to young patrons with outdoor interests by offering ballooning, jeep excursions, mountain climbing, and gourmet meals with optional vegetarian fare.

The resort hotel genre will no doubt continue to reflect contemporary concerns of the architectural profession. Changes will be embodied in the familiar cycle in which a trend-setting hotel presents new architectural and social possibilities and ideas, and in turn inspires numerous spin-offs and variations in subsequent hotels, until yet another trend-setter appears.

The characteristics of grand resort hotels which resorters have found appealing through a century and a half of enormous cultural change will no doubt remain valid for some time to come.

MIAMI BEACH

Florida, 1950s

Following the austere years of World War II Miami Beach was ready for a renaissance, and its second prosperous and spectacular era as a resort began. Americans had money to spend on vacations and were in search not only of sun and surf but of a setting that suggested all the luxury that had been missing since the beginning of the Great Depression.

As soon as restrictions on materials were lifted, new hotels were built in Miami Beach, bigger and far more lavish than those of the late 1930s and reminiscent of the larger hotels of the 1920s. In this postwar era, the resort city of Miami Beach shed all its pretensions to a Mediterranean architectural heritage and embraced a sensuous version of the austere and pristine International Style. Morris Lapidus is the man most associated with the postwar developments in Miami Beach. Of the many hotels he designed, the one that stands out as the most influential resort building of the 1950s is the Fontainebleau, a remarkable synthesis of site, style, clientele, and architectural vision that made it one of the most memorable in the world.

Lapidus completed a Beaux-Arts architectural education in 1927 with every intention of becoming a theatrical set designer. Such work being scarce, he pursued an architectural career designing retail shops in New York City during the 1930s and 1940s. He soon developed a reputation for innovative shop designs, experimenting in the use of color, light, and curvilinear forms to attract and move people through spaces. Immediately following World War II, Lapidus was given the opportunity to put his experience to use designing new facilities at Grossinger's and at the Concord Hotel in the Catskill Mountains of Sullivan County, New York.

During the late nineteenth century, mountain resorts popular with New York's Eastern European Jewish immigrants had earned the nickname "the Borscht Belt" for parts of the Poconos, the Berkshires, and especially Sullivan County. By providing good food and the setting for making a good match or an advantageous social contact, a small farm boardinghouse like Grossinger's could prosper and grow into a large resort hotel. The people attracted to these resorts were mostly from the Lower East Side of Manhattan, the Bronx, and Brooklyn. They were

The spacious dining terrace at the Eden Roc Hotel was one element that presaged a glamorous Miami Beach vacation.

urban people who conceived of vacations as a time for enjoying the company of family and friends; the wilderness, as such, held little appeal for them. Since the 1920s, life in the Borscht Belt resorts had centered on organized group activities and theatrical entertainments. Lapidus noticed, or rather rediscovered, that resorters in such a scenic setting had no desire to rough it—quite the opposite. They were dressing up in their best bib and tucker and promenading through the lobby and grounds and up and down grand staircases. What was called for, in his view, was not a rustic lodge but an urbane and even theatrical stage set that encouraged the guests to display their finery. The success of his work proved him right.

Lapidus' first hotel commission in Miami Beach was to design the main interior spaces of the Sans Souci Hotel in 1949. An over-all design had been established, and he was asked only to design the public spaces—the lobby, dining room, bar, and lounges. Again, his opulent stage-set interiors were an instant success. He was called upon to redesign the public spaces of five other hotels, including the Algiers and the Nautilus. These early efforts fulfilled the fantasies of a generation of people who had been raised in the Depression and whose clearest notions of elegance and luxury came out of the movies. Relying upon his early work and using color, light, curvilinear forms, and lavish materials, Lapidus created dramatic stairways, eclectic decorative schemes, and flattering illumination. All these elements were in the service of his fundamental goal: to provide a setting that made the guest feel like a millionaire or a movie star.

The Fontainebleau Hotel opened in 1953 to instant public acclaim. Everything about the place was extraordinary and on a scale not seen since the heyday of the 1920s. The lobby in particular was like a Busby Berkeley movie set of the 1930s. The building embodied a subtle blend of traditional and modern images. Owner Ben Novack had felt that a completely modern design would make the hotel look too austere and unappealing. He preferred the feeling of a French Renaissance building, but was not interested in an authentic copy. Lapidus discovered that French Renaissance forms and details, when simplified, fitted in rather well with modern ones. Thus, the Fontainebleau displayed an ornamental richness in an atmosphere that was contemporary. The public spaces were elaborately furnished with white and gold French antiques, crystal chandeliers, and a good deal of gilt. These same interiors employed changes of level to afford opportunities for dramatic movement—the chance to be on stage. Referring to the

Looking to the south, with the Fontainebleau and the Eden Roc in the foreground

circular marble stairway in the lobby, and the entrance to the dining room, the architect recalls:

There's a card room up there—that's all. All people ever do is walk halfway up, turn around and walk back down again. But they love that stairway. And they've seen it in the movies—the princess walks down the stairway.

To get into the dining room you walk up three steps, open a pair of doors and walk out on a platform, and then walk down three steps. Now the dining room is exactly the same level as my lobby, but as they walk up they reach the platform. I've got soft light lighting this thing up, and before they're seated, they are on stage as if they had been cast for the part. Everybody's looking at them; they're looking at everybody else.

On the exterior, the hotel was wholly modern. Its simple curved form gave a dynamic sweep both to the exterior and to the public spaces and a sense of enclosure to the gardens at the rear, which parodied French baroque models in flowers of red, white, and blue. Curving corridors on the guest-room floors visually eliminated the oppressive length often associated with long straight hallways. A low building paralleling the ocean and containing cabanas was serpentine in shape, a form not historically inspired but drawn from contemporary experiments with thin-shelled concrete structures.

Critics dismissed the hotel as "nouveau riche" and "kitsch," but the public loved the place. And the architect felt justifiably proud:

I've given these people something to gape at. You might call it a tasteful three-ring circus ... I gave it the luxurious once over where it shows. If I

Left: The Sans Souci Hotel, seen in 1950
Above: The rococo entrance to its dining room

put money in there, you saw it, and you can be sure everyone else will, too. I think I've struck something.

Indeed, he had discovered exactly the right mix of tradition and modernity, of image and efficiency, for the postwar era. The $13,000,000 Fontainebleau Hotel became _the_ model for the expensive luxury hotels of the 1950s and early 1960s. Lapidus went on to design a series of very good resort hotels in Miami and in the Caribbean, but the Fontainebleau remains his masterpiece.

Lapidus' next design was for the Eden Roc hotel, built next-door to the Fontainebleau in 1955. There he developed many of the ideas introduced in his earlier works. The Eden Roc too had a richly decorated yet wholly contemporary exterior. Inside, many period styles were freely adapted in the service of elegance. Once again, the architect planned everything from the kitchens to the bellboys' uniforms to the mirrors in the elevators that allowed the "performer" to straighten his tie or smooth her hair before appearing in the lobby.

For his Americana Hotel in nearby Bal Harbour, Lapidus adopted as a theme stylized symbols of twenty-one nations of the Western Hemisphere carried out in modern works of art and

Left, above: The Fontainebleau Hotel seen from its gardens
Left, below: The circular marble stairway in its lobby
Above: A smaller but no less flamboyant hotel of the period

The formal gardens, Olympic-sized swimming pool, beach, and sun decks of the Fontainebleau Hotel

elaborate decoration. The traditional guest-room slab was modified by the addition of angled balconies that created a zigzag pattern. Zigzag forms were also used in the plan of the low lanai wing and for the man-made landscape of the pool deck, separated from the natural beach by a row of cabanas. The main lobby is a long, low, two-story space freely disposed about a terrarium 35 feet in diameter and 40 feet high. This captive landscape is embellished with artificial moonlight and with tropical rainstorms scheduled to occur at two-hour intervals. There is an amusing irony in creating an indoor landscape in a region blessed with bountiful natural features.

In the 1960s and 1970s, Miami Beach was eclipsed by other resorts. It became, in a sense, a victim of its own success. The pattern of development that encouraged hotel after hotel to be constructed right on the beach ultimately had to be viewed as a failure. The beach itself, dependent upon but subdivided by little stone breakwaters into postage-stamp bits of sand, became shrouded with deep, dark afternoon shadows cast by the high-rise hotels jammed along Collins Avenue.

But even such flagrant destruction of its natural amenities was not, in the end, what diminished Miami Beach as a resort. More undermining was its inability to attract a new, affluent, and trendy crowd of vacationers. The South Beach area, developed in the 1930s with still-handsome streamlined, stucco-clad hotels, continues to attract the same people who have always gone there, though by now, of course, they are much older. The typical habitué of this area is a full-time resident living on retirement benefits and social security. Many of the hotels have become their permanent residences. The hotels designed by Lapidus and others in the 1950s also have continued to draw the same people year after year. The young, moneyed, trendy crowd of resorters has gone elsewhere.

It's not neat anymore to go back home and say you've been to Miami Beach, for example. The reason is Miami Beach hasn't changed in 10 or 15 years. It's stopped becoming more interesting.

That same article in the Miami Herald also observed:

If change is the life blood of a vibrant resort economy, then Boca Raton might easily capture the riches of the more affluent South Florida vacationers in the years ahead.

Thus Boca Raton, a resort to the north of Miami Beach that had

The entrance to the Eden Roc embodied images of elegance in the 1950s.

Left: An intimate bar in the Eden Roc (above) contrasts with the hotel's spectacular lobby (below).
Above: A terrarium is the centerpiece of the Americana Hotel's lobby.

been a kind of quaint backwater since the 1920s, is rethinking its future and renewing its investments, to its credit and success.

In addition to a lively convention trade, Miami Beach now caters primarily to two groups of vacationers, one much older than the other, who are loyal to the place and genuinely enjoy it. Some of the hotels, especially the Fontainebleau and the Eden Roc, look almost as good and are as much fun as ever. But still, it cannot be said that Miami Beach represents the cutting edge in resort trends. Of course, the town may yet make another comeback, though this will be harder than before. The 1970s is a time when many people equate a splendid vacation with almost reclusive privacy and the enjoyment of the offerings of the natural environment. For the moment, Miami Beach, with its urban density and squandered resources, seems the antithesis of the best resorts of the present day.

LAS VEGAS

Nevada

Las Vegas is perhaps the most fascinating and compelling American resort of the late twentieth century. It has been variously described as "Glitter Gulch," "Disneyland for Adults," "The Last of the Old Frontiers," and "The Land of Sodom and Gomorrah." From a distance, the neon city seems like something from a dream as it rises from the austere beauty of the desert. But desert landscapes, clean air, and healthy outdoor activities under perpetually sunny skies are not what people come here for. Most vacationers are drawn to Las Vegas by its livelier indoor features: gambling, all-star shows, and a high-rolling life-style. The rapid flow of vast amounts of money across the gaming tables and the presence of big-name nightclub entertainers that gambling subsidizes give Las Vegas a glamour all its own.

The development of Las Vegas as a fast-paced, glittering urban vacation spot is a relatively recent phenomenon. The barrenness of the desert made it a place unlikely to attract settlers interested in agriculture, even though there was plenty of local water from artesian wells and a high water table. The climate seemed far too harsh. The town was established in 1905 as a division point for the Los Angeles, San Pedro, and Salt Lake Railroad. The arrival of the Union Pacific Railroad, and the construction of Hoover Dam from 1928 to 1936, stimulated growth and even the construction of a modest hotel. But even though the state legislature had legalized gambling as early as 1931, Las Vegas did not become a resort town until after World War II.

Early efforts to promote tourism did not emphasize gambling. Las Vegas was touted as an ideal base from which to tour the beautiful Southwest, which was then very much in vogue. A chamber of commerce brochure published in 1940, entitled "Las Vegas, Nevada: Still a Frontier Town," listed Zion National Park, Death Valley, Lake Mead, Hoover Dam, and the Grand Canyon as nearby scenic wonders. The brochure pictured cowboys, a rodeo, a race track, hotels, auto courts, prospectors, a couple getting a divorce, a saloon with can-can girls—even a house of prostitution. In 1947, a Las Vegas booster described the town as having "the impact of a Wild West show, the friendliness of a country store, and the sophistication of Monte Carlo." In these early postwar years, the resort was promoted as a unique blend of the old and new:

The daunting and extraordinary Las Vegas Strip—a neon city in the austere desert

Where else under the sun could you see bearded prospectors leading their
burros in from the desert frontier...and in the evening mix with your favorite movie stars in brilliant casinos? You'll rub elbows with cowboys and
miners and be thrilled by famous entertainers in luxurious nightspots. Las
Vegas is truly the meetingplace of the old and new west, the smart playground of Hollywood and New York, the world's greatest combination of fun
and sun.

By the early 1950s, the developers of Las Vegas had sensed the
real potential of the place. It was not long before the old prospector
and the wonders of the desert landscape became passé and the
town acquired a different sort of image. An article in Argosy in
1948 had described the resort as

so wide open it makes the Grand Canyon look like a drainage ditch. It's
probably the crap-shootingest, hard-drinkingest, and high-livingest town in
these United States since San Francisco's Barbary Coast shut up shop
toward the end of the last century.

In the late 1960s, Joan Didion expressed her fascination with Las
Vegas, calling it

the most extreme and allegorical of American settlements, bizarre and
beautiful in its venality and in its devotion to immediate gratification, a
place the tone of which is set by mobsters and call girls and ladies room
attendants with amyl nitrite poppers in their uniform pockets.

The first fairly luxurious resort hotels in Las Vegas had appeared

Above: Fremont Street early in this century
Right: The same street today

in the early 1940s. But the establishment that really set the tone for the future was the Flamingo Hotel, built in 1946 for gangster Bugsy Siegal, who realized just what a gold mine legalized gambling and sex for sale could be. Siegal, alas, wasn't allowed to enjoy his new success; a year later, his bullet-riddled body was found in a Beverly Hills mansion. Nevertheless, he must be viewed as a far-sighted entrepreneur. The success of his Flamingo Hotel led ultimately to the construction of a whole flock of competitors. In a single decade, the Las Vegas "Strip," formerly known as the Los Angeles Highway, sprouted the Thunderbird Hotel (1948), Wilbur Clark's Desert Inn (1950), the Riviera Hotel (1955), the Sahara Hotel (1956), and the Sands Hotel (1956). In an effort to keep up, the Last Frontier, built in 1942, was extensively remodeled in 1955 and renamed the New Frontier, a name later shortened to simply the Frontier.

All of the major hotels in Las Vegas are alike in several respects. Without exception, the casino is billed as the primary attraction. The hotel floor plan is artfully contrived to lead patrons directly into the casino upon entering the building. Invariably, guests must walk past slot machines and gaming tables to reach the elevators, restaurants, and show rooms. Except for the ebb and flow of the crowds, the atmosphere inside the casino is timeless; neither clocks nor natural light are admitted to remind gamblers of the passage of time. The largest hotels are designed to eliminate any need and discourage any desire to leave the premises at all. They offer a variety of shops, restaurants, recreational and entertainment facilities, and the illusion that wealth is only a spin of the wheel away. Yet in fact, most visitors move from casino to casino, for a change of atmosphere, to catch a big-name entertainer at the dinner show, and to cruise through the neon night in hopes that their luck will be greater a mile down the Strip.

Although the attractions of Las Vegas as a whole are unique, the individual hotels provide virtually identical facilities and programs. So, in an effort to distinguish themselves from one another, grand hotels and modest motels alike each assume a recognizable image based upon a theme which they project through architecture and signs. This competitive attempt to make a distinctive statement along the visually congested Strip has resulted in a rich and vivid world of architectural imagery.

Interestingly, the early hotels were designed in a sensuous, streamlined version of the International Style, reflecting the concept of elegance characteristic of their time. The Sands, the Dunes, and the Riviera are three of the most successful examples of this type and show the influence of such Miami Beach hotels as the Fontainebleau. Each of them was conceived as an oasis in the

desert, an image achieved through the use of sand-colored stone and stucco cladding and the creation of lushly planted courtyards complete with songbirds and swimming pools. When compared with their more exuberant successors, these hotels seem remarkably subdued. Even additions made in the 1960s, such as the high-rise portions of the Sands and the Dunes, are straightforward modern structures.

The later hotels, representing a far larger monetary investment, are much more extravagantly baroque in atmosphere, use of materials, and architectural detailing. Whereas the early Las Vegas resort hotel offered a chic setting for gambling and revelry, the design of the building never completely excluded references to the desert and to the benign climate. By contrast, more recent hotels provide the guest with extraordinarily complete and self-contained fantasy environments.

On a scale far grander than ever before in Las Vegas, Caesar's Palace opened to the public in 1966. Designed by Melvin Grossman of Miami Beach, it offers the guest a resort environment based on a florid version of decadent upper-class life in ancient Rome. By focusing so completely on this illusion, the hotel becomes even more of an oasis, set apart from the desert landscape and from its blander competitors. From the Strip, a gigantic temple-shaped sign announces the daily attraction in the Caesar's Theater, appropriately named the Circus Maximus. A Carrara marble copy of the Victory of Samothrace guards the driveway, and behind her stretches a long pool of water punctuated by three fountains. Two rows of imported cypress trees complete this very formal and splendid approach. Marble copies of other ancient and Renaissance sculpture, including the Venus de Milo and Michelangelo's David, all scaled to be equal in height, flank the doorway. The scale, the opulence, and even the vulgarity of the place all contribute to the excitement of being there.

The building itself is wholly modern, though heavily ornamented to suggest Roman ancestry. The tall central portion is a convex slab faced with an openwork screen of grey concrete. At night, this façade is illuminated with soft aqua-blue light, causing the hotel to resemble a set from the 1937 movie Lost Horizons. Later additions are in the same style, but have badly altered the formal relationship between the driveway and the building. The colonnaded concave wings that flank the taller main building are articulated by sleek modern columns that owe allegiance to no ancient order. The Roman architectural theme exists only as surface decoration, and it is a mixed metaphor at best. As further thematic embellishment, Caesar's romance with Cleopatra was sufficient reason to introduce Egyptian references. Cleopatra's Barge, a floating

cocktail lounge, is meant to recall the boats that sailed the Nile in ancient times. The replica, outfitted with oars and furled sails, is closer to a Hollywood notion of its ancient Egyptian model than it is to the real thing. But then, the real thing—a rude wooden vessel—would hardly conjure up the festive atmosphere required by people on vacation. Not related to Caesar, but included nevertheless with an ease that seems particularly American, is a Japanese restaurant set in an interior garden complete with a waterfall and streams that meander beneath picturesque arched bridges.

Caesar's Palace is significantly different from previous Las Vegas hotels. It is very much bigger than the others; much of its impact is based on sheer size. Its layout is carefully worked out and shows a comprehensible sense of order, whereas previous hotels were planned in a deliberately informal and almost amorphously abstract way. And the architectural character of the hotel is brilliantly and overwhelmingly baroque.

Behind all the imagery and illusion, however, is a well-run first-class hotel, offering 1,200 rooms and a great number of recreational and entertainment facilities in a 35-acre complex. The guest seeking an even greater degree of luxury and escape from the everyday can arrange for a suite with a circular bed, mirrored ceiling, and sunken bathtub, or even for "the only two-story, six-bedroom suites in the world."

The Aladdin Hotel presents another fully developed exotic architectural image. The combination of Moorish, Persian, Arabian, and Indian themes may seem casual or even haphazard, but the result is breathtaking. The entrance portico alludes to Persia through the use of gilded columns, tiles, and other reflective surfaces that create the same golden, dazzling effect be it noon or midnight. Inside, the shopping arcade suggests an Oriental bazaar with its patterned rugs, tile floor, and flying-carpet draperies. By contrast, behind the Oriental casino stand the original guest wings, which were designed in a mock-Tudor style.

Some Las Vegas hotels have a visual character established, not by the architecture itself, but rather by signs: decorations and logos applied to the surfaces of a forthright contemporary building or placed out at the roadway. An exceedingly conventional Holiday Inn rises behind a casino built in the shape of a whimsical illuminated steamboat, complete with costumed figures on its bow. At the Stardust Hotel, the theme is embodied in the glittering sign which, at night, imitates a shower of stars through a blue and purple sky. These colors and motifs are repeated across the long, low façade of the building. The entry portico is a shining silver-

The vast casino of the MGM Grand Hotel is far bigger than a football field.

metal structure with extraterrestrial overtones. On the interior, the same dazzling night sky is achieved by means of the same dark shades of color and flickering white lights, whose effect is multiplied by mirrors.

The casino of the Circus Circus hotel, built in 1968, resembles a tremendous pink-and-white-striped circus tent. It is unique in Las Vegas in that it appeals to families with children. The casino and bars are located on the ground floor, while above, balconies containing live circus acts, skill games, and side-show attractions permit youngsters and nongamblers to be removed from yet keep in view of the activity in the casino below.

The original Flamingo Hotel of 1946 was one of the first establishments on what was to become the Las Vegas Strip. Since its acquisition by the Hilton Hotels Corporation in 1971, the Flamingo has been given a dynamic new appearance. A band of pearly pink flamingos on a mirrored background marches across the front of the building. The hotel makes the most of its corner location with a spectacular sign shaped to resemble a flamingo's tail. Its flamelike form and brilliant, changeable pink coloring make it one of the most distinctive and truly beautiful light displays on the Strip.

The MGM Grand Hotel, designed by Martin Stern, is one of the newest, largest, and grandest hotels on the Las Vegas Strip. Seen in its entirety, it is a wholly modern, even futuristic high-rise structure. Its twenty-six-story height is enlivened and visually lightened by the use of reflective glass in the upper tiers. Yet despite the modernity of its over-all image, there is nothing austere about the MGM Grand. The Las Vegas investment company that purchased Metro-Goldwyn-Mayer Studios a few years ago chose the golden days of Hollywood as the theme for their hotel. The guest is immersed in recognizable fragments of a movie-set fantasy. The desert landscape is overshadowed by the far more appealing imaginary landscape of Hollywood. By ignoring the desert site in favor of a self-contained, make-believe world, the MGM Grand follows the tradition established by Caesar's Palace over a decade earlier.

The three doorways into the hotel are covered by curved gables suggesting a pagoda roof. The fountain at the parking-lot level is an early-twentieth-century copy of a seventeenth-century work: Lorenzo Giambologna's Neptune and the Sirens. The piece was executed in 1913, but remained unsold until it was acquired for the MGM Grand. The simple wrought-iron balustrade adjacent to the fountain ends rather startlingly in oversized gilded cartouches. This same mixture of stupefying scale and free architectural character appears elsewhere in the hotel.

On the interior, any attempt at restrained modernism has been

Right, above: The Aladdin Hotel and the MGM Grand Hotel beyond. Each of these huge hotels contains an interior fantasy world that stands in stark contrast to the natural world of the desert.
Right, below: The approach to the MGM Grand Hotel

completely abandoned. The lobby and casino are decorated in dark red and black, with large crystal chandeliers overhead. Ionic pilasters and classicizing statues ornament the hallways and lobby. The MGM Grand is one of the few hotels in Las Vegas where patrons do not enter directly into the casino; rather, the reception desk, elevators, and restaurants are elevated slightly above the casino level. The vast size of the casino—it is almost one-and-a-half times the length of a football field—and its position several steps below the lobby make it seem more expansive, less congested, and more appealing than its competitors.

The guest rooms, too, diverge from the building's contemporary exterior. They are decorated with velvet bedspreads and curtains, shag rugs, and "French Provincial" furniture. Some are equipped with a luxurious bathroom almost as large as the bedroom itself, with sunken tub and mirrored walls.

Two motifs repeated throughout the hotel serve to remind the visitor of the MGM connection. The lion's-head logo appears on rugs, elevator doors, and all the hotel's paper products, and in the presence of a real lion who spends part of the day in the shopping arcade sitting for portraits with guests. Movie stars, too, are everywhere. Poster-sized photographs of past and present stars decorate the corridors and the delicatessen restaurant. Plaster masks preserve their features and a movie theater showing only MGM classics brings them to life. A gold star on every guest-room door encourages patrons to think of themselves as part of the gallery of famous faces.

The MGM Grand is the only hotel in Las Vegas to have two showrooms—the stage in the Ziegfeld Room rises out of the floor and can hold as many as 667 "scantily clad showgirls." The jai alai fronton is the only one in the world associated with a hotel, and the shopping arcade is the largest anywhere within a hotel. In its proud listing of "firsts," "biggests," and "onlys," the hotel management is behaving exactly like its nineteenth-century predecessors.

Las Vegas is the ultimate fantasy resort of the late twentieth century. It is true that the city is the only one in the world where service stations, often viewed as the epitome of garish commercialism, are lost amid the far more colorful, vibrant, and spectacular display of the hotels and casinos. Yet for all its brazenness, Las Vegas is a fantasy world that may be compared to Disneyland—on a grown-up scale. Set in a landscape that seems to heighten the sense of isolation from the "real" world, it provides a specialized environment where the most sedate visitors can shed their inhibitions and feel sinfully wild and daring as they sample forbidden delights—however vicariously—or risk their fortunes on the gaming tables.

MAUNA KEA

Island of Hawaii, Hawaiian Islands

One of the most interesting and influential resort hotels of recent years is the Mauna Kea on the big island of Hawaii. It is one of the few hotels where a wholly modern style of architecture has been used to create a place that is at once festive, elegant, and open to the advantages of climate and landscape.

With the exception of the sea and sandy beach, the 500-acre site was not the lush tropical paradise that most people expect of Hawaii. The arid lava soil with its sparse vegetation was desertlike when Laurance Rockefeller decided to develop it as one of his world-wide chain of resorts. Irrigation and lavish planting around the building have made the setting appear more like the Mainlander's image of Hawaii. Even so, nearly two-thirds of the site has been left in its natural state.

After experimenting with a "village" theme for the site, architects Charles Bassett and Marc Goldstein of Skidmore, Owings and Merrill, San Francisco, developed an attractive alternative to the usual tall, simple box. The rooms are arranged in two low, stepped slabs, which are set apart at ground level and step toward each other on the higher floors. This forms a long, pyramidal open-air atrium with rows of rooms hovering above. The atrium, luxuriantly landscaped, contains some of the public spaces.

Entry to the hotel is across a bridge into the reception area, situated on a floating platform punctuated with openings to reveal the gardens below. Instead of lining dark corridors, the rooms are reached by open balconies that overlook the reception area and gardens. The main level of the hotel is really a series of terraces stepped down the hillside toward the beach through abundant planting. The bar, auditorium, shops, and offices are conceived more as shallow caves than as normal rooms. The wood-framed dining pavilion is similarly terraced to assure each diner a view of the surf. Its wicker-shaded glass walls stand open most of the time, but are ready to slide shut at the approach of a tropical shower. The service level is buried unobtrusively below ground, while the guest rooms are suspended overhead between graceful cross-shaped columns, like a giant sheltering beach umbrella.

Nature is the most important attraction at the Mauna Kea, and nothing in the building is allowed to detract from it. The guest can enjoy the natural qualities of

In its landscaped central atrium, the hotel lobby is seen below and the guest rooms above, connected by bridges.

The Mauna Kea Hotel and its broad crescent-shaped beach

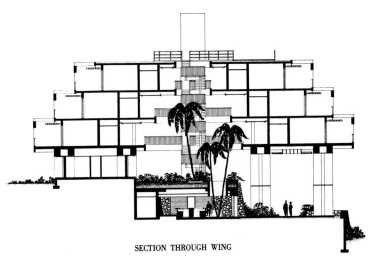

SECTION THROUGH WING

Above: The cross section shows the guest rooms, each with a balcony, on each side of the central garden atrium.   Left: An interior, with folk art used as decoration

the place while still retaining a sense of shelter and privacy. To give the building an atmosphere of quiet, the architects adhered to a limited range of materials. The outer walls are of concrete painted a soft cream color, and the floors are of flagstone or tile. The inner walls are of a subtly textured plaster, and the ceiling and all the woodwork are of deep brown Nara wood.

The Mauna Kea is pervaded by an air of monied ease, of subtle and casual luxury. Ostentation has no place there; a refined simplicity rules even the smallest details. There are no suites. Even the guest rooms are not overly large by the standards of other hotels, but because of the stepped arrangement of the building they all open onto balconies through sliding walls of glass and wooden shutters that allow the guest to do without air conditioning. From each balcony there is a view of the ocean or mountains. The interior decor of these rooms is disarmingly simple. Straw mats cover the tile floors. The furniture is light willow and cane. Brightly colored Haitian bedspreads harmonize with the Hawaiian flower prints that adorn the walls.

Works of art with a Polynesian flavor provide interest and splashes of color throughout the building. While some of the Hawaiian quilts are of museum quality, they are never allowed to dominate. At the Mauna Kea, the landscape and the sea are the heart of the experience. The contemplation and enjoyment of nature is an important part of the sophisticated pleasures of the Mauna Kea, as it was in a number of nineteenth-century resorts located similarly in a beautiful wilderness.

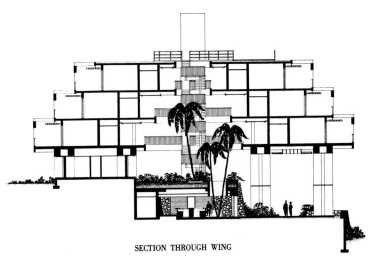

HOTEL TAHARA'A INTERCONTINENTAL

Papeete, Tahiti

The Hotel Tahara'a enjoys a magnificent cliffside site overlooking beautiful Matavai Bay and the island of Mooréa. The architects, Wimberly, Whisenand, Allison, Tong and Goo of Hawaii, stepped the guest rooms, each with a garden terrace, down the face of the cliff. Now that the planting has grown to blend with the thick vegetation of the hillside, the rooms are quite unobtrusive from the dining room, public spaces, and terraces on the plateau above. To give the building an appearance appropriate to Tahiti and appealing to the expectations of its predominantly American clientele, the architects applied conventional imagery drawn from Polynesian villages and from the mythology of the South Pacific.

An early view of the hotel shows the stepped terraces of guest rooms before they were camouflaged by the landscape.

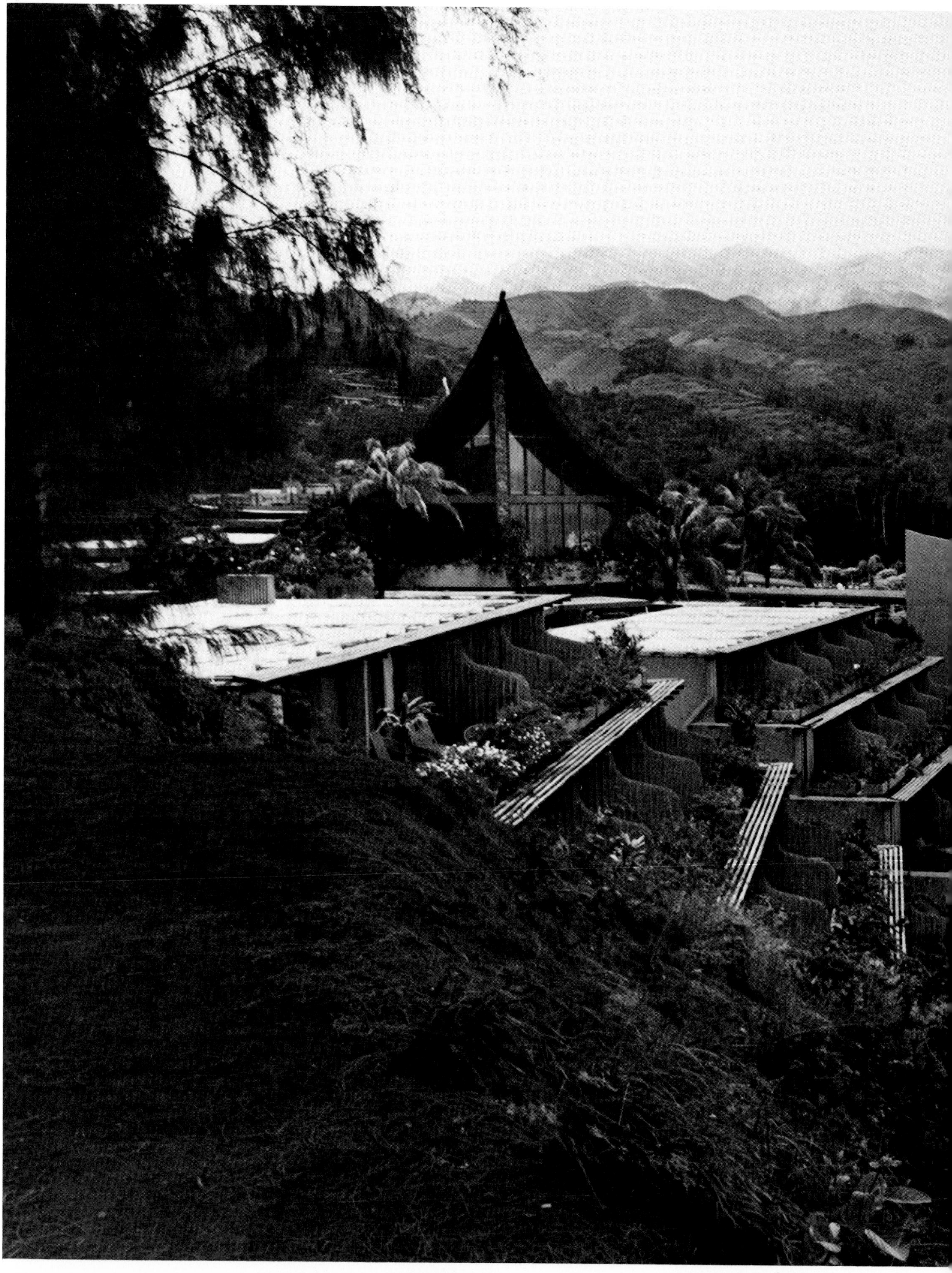

The guest rooms step down the cliff, allowing the hotel to merge visually with its site and creating terraces at the top with unencumbered views.

PLAYBOY
RESORT HOTEL
Lake Geneva, Wisconsin

Lake Geneva has long been a popular resort for Midwesterners, offering a wooded country environment only a short drive from Chicago and Milwaukee. It is no wonder that Playboy Clubs International chose to locate one of its large resort hotels here, not far from its international headquarters in Chicago.

The Playboy Resort Hotel, with its low horizontal forms, seems at home in its setting, an impression furthered by the use of rustic materials. The walls of exposed aggregate concrete are complemented by redwood balconies and roof fascias. This restrained palette used by architects Robert Taege and Associates gives the complex the air of a suburban corporate headquarters, well suited to the sophisticated, worldly image that the Playboy organization seeks to project.

KAH-NEE-TAH LODGE
Warm Springs, Oregon

The clean, clear air, perpetual sunshine, and rugged landscape of Oregon's inland desert are in marked contrast to the rainy weather and verdant landscape of its populous western coast. The Kah-Nee-Tah Lodge was built for the Confederated Tribes of Warm Springs Indians in order to capitalize on the attraction and in an effort to bring new jobs to their people.

The architects, Wolf-Zimmer-Gunsul-Frasca-Ritter, of Portland, Oregon, chose to design a building that contrasts with its site. Seen from a distance, Kah-Nee-Tah's forms are strongly geometric, yet the earthy yellow-brown of the cedar-board walls harmonizes with the colors of the landscape. The wings of the building shelter the courtyard and swimming-pool terrace from the powerful winds. The architects have made the most of the beauty of the simple cedar walls and heavy timber and concrete structure rather than relying on applied decoration for mood and character.

The lobby of the hotel, with its trusses that have both a structural and a decorative purpose

The hotel's geometrical forms stand in stark contrast to the desert landscape.

CAMINO REAL HOTEL
Cancún, Mexico

The resort island of Cancún on Mexico's Caribbean shore has been developing rapidly in the last few years. As a result, much of the sand-bar-and-lagoon-dotted terrain that attracted people in the first place is being transformed into yet another broad sandy beach lined with typical high-rise hotels. The Camino Real Hotel stands in impressive contrast to its mundane neighbors. Despite its 256 guest rooms, the complex, owned by the American-based Western International Hotels chain, manages to project a low-key, intimate atmosphere. Architect Ricardo Legoretta sensitively responded to and reinforced the character of the island by creating a beautiful turquoise-blue lagoon and placing his hotel's guest rooms, patios, gardens, and pools around it. The large guest-room wing forms a sheltering backdrop on a spit of land between the lagoon and the ocean, thus assuring every room of a view.

The rough, adobe-like walls and the abstract cubic masses of the architecture subtly recall traditional Mexican vernacular buildings. The pyramidal massing of the guest wing, with its cool garden atrium, suggests Mayan temples. The simple geometric forms of which the hotel is composed and the use of traditional Mexican materials such as raffia, rattan, wood, and ceramics in its interior give the Camino Real an air of simple, relaxed elegance and timeless beauty. Allusions to things Mexican come from the materials and construction of the building itself, rather than from applied decoration as in the hotels at Walt Disney World. The Camino Real is not only an efficient and economical building but a powerful piece of architecture as well, exemplary of the contemporary grand resort hotel at its best.

A detail of the exterior of the hotel from the lagoon shows the stepped form of the building, which gives each room a balcony.

The hotel's lagoon is in the foreground, with the island landscape of Cancún beyond.

The landscaped atrium of the hotel

The pool-side bar

AMERICA'S GRAND RESORT HOTELS

The Ahwahnee
Yosemite National Park,
California 95389
209 372-4671

Aladdin Hotel
3667 Las Vegas Boulevard South
Las Vegas, Nevada 89109
702 735-0111

Americana Hotel
9701 Collins Avenue
Bal Harbour, Florida 33154
305 865-7511

Arizona Biltmore
2400 E. Missouri Avenue
Phoenix, Arizona 85016
602 955-6600

The Balsams
Dixwell Notch, New Hampshire
603 255-3400

Belleview-Biltmore Hotel
Belleair, Florida
813 442-6171

Beverly Hills Hotel
9641 West Sunset Boulevard
Beverly Hills, California 90210
213 276-2251

Biscaya Retirement Hotel
(formerly Floridian Hotel)
540 West End Avenue
Miami Beach, Florida

Boca Raton Hotel and Club
(formerly Cloister Inn)
501 East Camino Real
Boca Raton, Florida 33432
305 395-3000

Boulevard Hotel
(now a retirement home)
775 Dade Boulevard
Miami Beach, Florida

The Breakers
P.O. Box 910
Palm Beach, Florida 33480
305 655-6611

The Broadmoor
Colorado Springs, Colorado 80901
303 634-7711

Caesar's Palace
3570 Las Vegas Boulevard South
Las Vegas, Nevada 89109
702 731-7110

Camino Real
Cancún, Mexico
D.F. 250-51-44
Cancún 3-01-00

Circus Circus
3645 Las Vegas Boulevard South
Las Vegas, Nevada 89109
702 735-0410

Hotel Colorado
526 Pine Street
Glenwood Springs,
Colorado 81601
303 945-6511

Hotel Del Coronado
1500 Orange Avenue
Coronado, California 92118
714 435-6611

Eden Roc Hotel
4525 Collins Avenue
Miami Beach, Florida 33140
305 532-2561

El Tovar
Grand Canyon National Park
Grand Canyon, Arizona 86023
602 638-2401

Flamingo Hotel
3555 Las Vegas Boulevard South
Las Vegas, Nevada 89109
702 735-0410

Fontainebleau Hotel
4441 Collins Avenue
Miami Beach, Florida 33140
305 538-8811

Glacier Park Hotel
East Glacier Park, Montana 59434
406 226-9311

Glenwood Hot Springs Lodge
526 Pine Street
Glenwood Springs, Colorado 81601
303 945-6571

Grand Hotel
Mackinac Island, Michigan 49757
906 847-3331

The Greenbrier
White Sulphur Springs,
West Virginia 24986
304 536-1110

Grove Park Inn
Asheville, North Carolina 28804
704 252-2711

The Homestead
Hot Springs, Virginia 24445
804 839-5500

Kah-Nee-Tah Vacation Resort
Warm Springs, Oregon 97761
800 425-1138

La Fonda Hotel
Santa Fe, New Mexico 87501
505 982-5511

Lake McDonald Lodge
West Glacier, Montana 59936
406 888-5431

Madonna Inn
100 Madonna Road
San Luis Obispo, California 93401
805 543-3000

Mauna Kea
Island of Hawaii, Hawaiian Islands
808 882-7222

Essex House
(designed by Henry Hohauser, 1938)
1001 Collins Avenue
Miami Beach, Florida 33139

New Yorker Hotel
(designed by Henry Hohauser, 1940)
1611 Collins Avenue
Miami Beach, Florida 33139

MGM Grand Hotel
3645 Las Vegas Boulevard South
Las Vegas, Nevada 89109
702 739-4111

Mission Inn
3649 Seventh Street
Riverside, California 92501
714 784-0300

Mohonk Mountain House
New Paltz, New York 12561
914 258-1000

Old Faithful Inn
Yellowstone National Park,
Wyoming 82190
307 344-7311

Paradise Inn
Mount Rainier National Park
Ashford, Washington 98304
206 569-2291

Playboy Resort and Country Club
Lake Geneva, Wisconsin 53147
414 248-8811

Royal Hawaiian Hotel
2259 Kalakaua Avenue
Honolulu, Hawaii 96815
808 923-7311

Sans Souci Hotel
3101 Collins Avenue
Miami Beach, Florida 33154
305 538-6861

Stardust Hotel
3000 Las Vegas Boulevard South
Las Vegas, Nevada 89109
702 736-6111

Santa Barbara Biltmore
Montecito, California 93108
805 969-2261

Tahara'a Intercontinental
Papeete, Tahiti

Timberline Lodge
Mount Hood, Oregon 97041
503 226-7979

Wentworth-by-the-Sea
New Castle, New Hampshire 03854
603 436-3100

Extant Converted Hotels

The Alcazar
Lightner Museum
City Hall, King Street
Saint Augustine, Florida 32084
904 829-9677

Hotel Del Monte
U.S. Naval Postgraduate School
Monterey, California 93940
408 646-2411

The Ponce de Leon
Flagler College
Saint Augustine, Florida 32084
904 824-2202

Hotel Rolyat
Stetson University College of Law
Saint Petersburg, Florida
813 345-1300

Tampa Bay Hotel
University of Tampa
401 West Kennedy Boulevard
Tampa, Florida
813 253-8861

Bibliography

Albert Pick-Barth Co. **Hotel Planning and Outfitting.** Chicago, 1928.

Alexander, Robert Crozier. **Ho! For Cape Island.** Cape May, N.J., 1956.

American Guide Series. **Entertaining a Nation: The Career of Long Branch, New Jersey,** Bayonne, N.J., 1940.

Amory, Cleveland. **The Last Resorts.** New York, 1952.

Andersen, Timothy; Moore, Eudorah M.; and Winter, Robert. **California Design 1910.** Pasadena, Calif., 1974.

Anderson, John, and Moore, Stearns. **The Book of the White Mountains.** New York, 1930.

Appalachian Mountain Club. **Guide to the White Mountains and Adjacent Regions.** Boston, 1925.

Appleton's Handbook of American Travel, Southern Tour. New York, 1873.

Appleton's Illustrated Handbook of American Winter Resorts: For Tourists and Invalids. New York, 1877.

Armbruster, Eugene L. **Coney Island.** New York, 1924.

Architectural Record: Motels, Hotels, Restaurants, and Bars. First edition, New York, 1953. Second edition, New York, 1960.

Armes, Manley. **The Book of Colorado Springs.** Colorado Springs, Colo., n.d.

Babcock, Louis. **Our American Resorts.** New York, 1884.

Bachelder, John B. **Bachelder's Popular Resorts and How to Reach Them.** Boston, 1874.

Baedecker, Karl. **The United States with an Excursion into Mexico.** New York, 1904.

Bancroft, Caroline. **Glenwood's Early Glamor.** Boulder, Colo., 1958.

Barnstone, Howard. **The Galveston That Was.** Houston, Texas, 1966.

Barrett, Richmond. **Good Old Summer Days.** New York, 1941.

Baur, John E. **The Health-Seekers of Southern California, 1870-1900.** San Marino, Calif., 1959.

Blake, Mary E. **On the Wing: Rambling Notes of a Trip to the Pacific.** Boston, 1883.

Bourbaki, Nicholas. **Fine Times in Fine Places: The Traveling Teetotaler Takes to the Trail.** Baltimore, 1885.

Bradley, Hugh. **Such Was Saratoga.** New York, 1940.

Bryant, William Cullen. **Picturesque America, or The Land We Live In.** New York, 1874.

Buckley, Marcie. **The Crown City's Brightest Gem.** Coronado, Calif., 1973.

Caesar's Palace. **This Is Caesar's Palace.** Descriptive brochure.

Cahan, Abraham. **The Rise of David Levinsky.** New York, 1966.

Clark, Susie C. **The Round Trip from the Hub to the Golden Gate.** New York, 1890.

Colman, Samuel (Mark Pencil). **The White Sulphur Papers on Life at the Springs of Western Virginia.** New York, 1839.

Curtis, George William. **Lotus-Eating: A Summer Book.** New York, 1856.

Dall, Caroline. **My First Holiday.** Boston, 1881.

Dallas. Sandra. **No More Than Five in a Bed: Colorado Hotels in the Old Days.** Norman, Okla., 1967.

Davidson, Marshall B. **Life in America.** Boston, 1951.

Delkin, James Ladd. **The Monterey Peninsula.** Sacramento, Calif., 1941.

De Veaux, S. **The Traveller's Own Book to Saratoga Springs, Niagara Falls and Canada.** Buffalo, N.Y., 1841 and 1845.

Didion, Joan. **Slouching Towards Bethlehem.** New York, 1968.

Dorsey, Leslie, and Devine, Janice. **Fare Thee Well.** New York, 1964.

End, Henry. **Interiors Book of Hotels and Motor Hotels.** New York, 1963.

_____ **Interiors Second Book of Hotels.** New York, 1978.

Evers, Alf. **The Catskills: From Wilderness to Woodstock.** Garden City, N.Y., 1972.

Feitz, Leland. **The Antlers: A Quick History of Colorado Springs' Historic Hotel.** Denver, Colo., 1972.

Frohman, Charles E. **Put-In-Bay.** Columbus, Ohio, 1971.

Funnell, Charles E. **By the Beautiful Sea: The Rise and High Times of That Great American Resort, Atlantic City.** New York, 1975.

Gadd, John. "Saltair, Great Salt Lake's Most Famous Resort." **Utah Historical Quarterly.** Summer 1968.

Gage, Emma Abbott. **Western Wanderings and Summer Saunterings Through Picturesque Colorado.** Baltimore, 1900.

Gale, Zona. **Frank Miller of the Mission Inn.** New York, 1938.

Gebhard, David. "The Alvarado Hotel." **New Mexico Architect,** November-December 1964.

_____ . "Architecture and the Fred Harvey Houses." **New Mexico Architect,** July-August 1962.

_____ . "Architecture and the Fred Harvey Houses." **New Mexico Architect,** January-February 1964.

_____ . **George Washington Smith.** Santa Barbara, Calif., 1964.

Geiger, Helen M. **The Broadmoor Story.** Colorado Springs, Colo., 1968.

Gill, Brendan, and Witney, Dudley. **Summer Places.** New York, 1978.

Gillman, Lucy P. "Coney Island." **New York History,** July 1955.

Girouard, Mark. **Sweetness and Light.** New York, 1977.

Golovin, Ivan. **Stars and Stripes.** New York, 1856.

Govan, Gilbert E., and Livingood, James W. **The Chattanooga Country.** Chapel Hill, N.C., 1963.

Gowans, Alan. **Images of American Living: Four Centuries of Architecture and Furniture as Cultural Expression.** New York, 1964.

Graham, Thomas. "Flagler's Magnificent Hotel Ponce de Leon." **Florida Historical Quarterly,** July 1975.

Hamlin, Talbot. **Greek Revival Architecture in America.** New York, 1944.

Harris, Neil, ed. **The Land of Contrasts, 1880-1901.** New York, 1970.

Heimer, Mel. **Fabulous Bawd: The Story of Saratoga.** New York, 1952.

Henderson, James D. "Meals by Fred Harvey: A Phenomenon of the American West." Unpublished master's thesis, Temple University, 1965.

Hepburn, Andrew. **The Great Resorts of North America.** New York, 1965.

Hill, Ralph Nading. **Lake Champlain — Key to Liberty.** Taftsville, Vt., 1977.

Hoffman, Donald. **The Architecture of John Wellborn Root.** Baltimore, 1973.

Howells, William Dean. **The Rise of Silas Lapham.** New York, 1963.

Hutchings, DeWitt V. **Handbook of the Mission Inn.** Riverside, Calif., 1951.

Ingersoll, Ernest. **Down East Latch Strings.** Boston, 1887.

Ivers, Louise H. "The Montezuma Hotel at Las Vegas Hot Springs, New Mexico." **Journal of the Society of Architectural Historians,** October 1974.

James, Henry. **The American Scene.** Bloomington, Ind., 1968.

Johnson, Alva. **The Legendary Mizners.** New York, 1953.

Jones, Howard Mumford. **The Age of Energy: Varieties of American Experience, 1865-1915.** New York, 1970.

Kalman, Harold D. **The Railway Hotels and the Development of the Chateau Style in Canada.** Victoria, B.C., 1968.

Kaufmann, Perry. "City Boosters Las Vegas Style." **Journal of the West,** 1971.

Kinney, Henry. **Once Upon a Time: The Legend of the Boca Raton Hotel and Club.** Boca Raton, Fla., 1966.

Klotz, Esther. **Riverside the Day the Bank Broke.** Riverside, Calif., 1972.

Kobbe, Gustav. **The New Jersey Coast and Pines.** Short Hills, N.C., 1889.

Lancaster, Clay. **Architectural Follies in America.** Rutland, Vt., 1960.

Langley, Joan and Wright. **Yesterday's Asheville.** Miami, Fla., 1975.

Lardner, Ring. **The Ring Lardner Reader.** Ed. Maxwell Geismar. New York, 1963.

Leavengood, David. "The Yellowstone Park Hotels of Robert Reamer." **Mountain Gazette** (Denver, Colo.), 1974.

Leavitt, Richard F. **Yesterday's New Hampshire.** Miami, Fla., 1974.

Limerick, Jeffrey W. "The Grand Resort Hotels of America." **Perspecta 15: The Yale Architectural Journal,** 1975.

McAllister, Ward. **Society As I Have Found It.** New York, 1890.

MacFadden, Harry Alexander. **Rambles in the West.** Hollidaysburg, Pa., 1906.

McGinty, Brian. **The Palace Inns: A Connoisseur's Guide to Historic American Hotels.** New York: Two Continents Publishing Group, 1978.

Margolies, John. **Morris Lapidus: Architecture of Joy.** New York, 1970.

Marnell, William H. **Vacation Yesterdays of New England.** New York, 1975.

Martin, Sidney W. **Florida's Flagler.** Athens, Ga., 1949.

Monroe, Harriet. **John Wellborn Root: A Study of His Life and Work.** Park Forest, Ill., 1966.

Moore, Charles W. "You Have to Pay for the Public Life." **Perspecta 9–10: The Yale Architectural Journal,** 1965.

Morris, George W. **Glimpses of the Great Pleasure Resorts of New England.** Portland, Maine, 1895.

——. **Scenic Gems of Maine.** Portland, Maine, 1898.

Morris, Mrs. James Edwin. **A Pacific Coast Vacation.** New York, 1901.

Muir, John. **Letters to a Friend, 1866-1879.** Boston, 1915.

Nash, Roderick. **Wilderness and the American Mind.** New Haven, Conn., 1967.

Newcomb, Rexford. **Mediterranean Domestic Architecture in the United States.** Cleveland, Ohio, 1928.

O'Connor, Richard. **The Golden Summers: An Antic History of Newport.** New York, 1974.

Olcott, William. **The Greenbrier Heritage.** The Greenbrier, White Sulphur Springs, Va.

Olson, Arlene R. **A Guide to the Architecture of Miami Beach.** Miami, Fla., 1978.

Pevsner, Nikolaus. **A History of Building Types.** Princeton, N.J., 1976.

Platt, Frederick. **America's Gilded Age.** Cranbury, N.J., 1976.

Pomeroy, Earl. **In Search of the Golden West: The Tourist in Western America.** New York, 1957.

Raftery, A. H. **A Miracle in Hotel Building.** Yellowstone Park Company, n.d.

Reniers, Percival. **The Springs of Virginia.** Chapel Hill, N.C., 1941.

Rhodes, Harrison. **American Towns and People.** New York, 1920.

——. **In Vacation America.** New York, 1915.

Robbins, Mel. **Poland Spring — An Informal History.** Poland Spring, Maine, 1975.

Rockwell, Rev. Charles. **The Catskill Mountains and the Region Around.** New York, 1873.

Sanborn, Kate. **A Truthful Woman in Southern California.** New York, 1893.

Sanford, Trent Elwood. **The Architecture of the Southwest: Indian, Spanish, American.** New York, 1950.

Sargent, Shirley. **The Ahwahnee, Yosemite's Classic Hotel.** Yosemite, Calif., 1977.

Sexton, Randolph. **Spanish Influence on American Architecture and Decoration.** New York, 1927.

Sheine, James. **Glacier National Park Historic Resources Study.** National Park Service, 1970.

Sklar, Robert, ed. **The Plastic Age: 1917-1930.** New York, 1970.

Smiley, Nixon. **Yesterday's Florida.** Miami, Fla., 1974.

Smyth, George Hutchinson. **The Life of Henry Bradley Plant.** New York, 1898.

Spencer, Wilma Bell. **Palm Beach: A Century of Heritage.** Washington, 1975.

Staats, W. Philip. **California Architecture in Santa Barbara.** New York, 1929.

Stevens, Lewis T. **The History of Cape May County.** Cape May City, N.J., 1897.

Stevenson, Robert Louis. **Across the Plains.** New York, 1895.

Stoddard, Seneca Ray. **Lake George and Lake Champlain.** Glens Falls, N.Y., 1906.

Stone, William L. **Reminiscences of Saratoga and Ballston.** New York, 1890.

Street, George G. **Che Wah Wah: The Montezuma Club in Mexico.** Chicago, 1883.

Stuart, James. **Three Years in North America.** Edinburgh, 1832.

Sweeney, Fred, and Wyatt, Richard. "Grand Hotels of California." Unpublished master's thesis, California Polytechnic State University, San Luis Obispo, Calif., 1974.

Taintor Brothers. **Taintor's Guide Books: Hudson River Route.** New York, 1881 and 1889.

Tarbell, Ida M. **The Florida Architecture of Addison Mizner.** New York, 1928.

Thomas, George E., and Doebley, Carl. **Cape May, Queen of the Seaside Resorts: Its History and Architecture.** Philadelphia, 1976.

Thompson, Deborah, ed. **Maine Forms of Architecture.** Camden, Maine, 1976.

Thompson, Hunter. **Fear and Loathing in Las Vegas.** New York, 1971.

University of Tampa. **A History of the Tampa Bay Hotel.** Tampa, Fla., 1966.

Van Orman, Richard A. **A Room for the Night: Hotels in the Old West.** New York, 1966.

Van Zandt, Roland. **The Catskill Mountain House.** New Brunswick, N.J., 1966.

Vaughan, Thomas, and Ferriday, Virginia. **Space, Style and Structure: Building in Northwest America.** Portland, Ore., 1974.

Veblen, Thorstein. **The Theory of the Leisure Class.** New York, 1953.

Waller, George. **Saratoga: Saga of an Impious Era.** Englewood Cliffs, N.J., 1966.

Weiss, Harry B., and Kemble, Howard R. **They Took to the Waters.** Trenton, N.J., 1962.

Weisskamp, Herbert. **Hotels: An International Survey.** New York, 1968.

Wharton, Edith. **The Custom of the Country.** New York, 1941.

Williamson, Jefferson. **The American Hotel: An Anecdotal History.** New York, 1930.

Willis, N. P. **American Scenery.** New York, 1838-1840.

Wilson, Blanche N. **The Minnetonka Story.** Minneapolis, Minn., 1971.

Wilson, Harold F. **The Story of the Jersey Shore.** Princeton, N.J., 1964.

Woodfill, W. Stewart. **Grand Hotel: The Story of an Institution.** New York, 1969.

Wright, Frank Lloyd **An Autobiography.** New York, 1932.

Miscellaneous travel, hotel, and local promotional pamphlets and brochures.

PERIODICALS AND NEWSPAPERS

· **American Architecture and Building News (American Architect)**
· **Architect and Engineer**
· **Architectural Record**
· **Architectural Review**
· **Art Quarterly**
· **Brick Builder (later Architectural Forum)**
· **Cornell Hotel and Restaurant Administration Quarterly**
· **Craftsman Magazine**
· **Frank Leslie's Weekly Illustrated Newspaper**
· **Harper's Monthly**
· **Harper's Weekly**
· **Historic Preservation**
· **Hotel Monthly**
· **Interiors**
· **Land of Sunshine**
· **Michigan Society of Architects Monthly Bulletin**
· **The Nation**
· **Out West**
· **Progressive Architecture**
· **Journal of the Society of Architectural Historians**
· **Sunset**
· **Western Architect**

Index

Underscored page numbers refer to illustrations.

Picture Credits